CAREER IN TRANSITION

101 LESSONS TO ACHIEVE JOB SEARCH SUCCESS

MARK BEAL & FRANK KOVACS

Published by Mark Beal Media, LLC
Toms River, New Jersey

Cover Design: Tahnee Sauer

ISBN: 9781687296900
First Printing: 2019 Printed in the United States of America

Career In Transition: 101 Lessons To Achieve Job Search Success is available for bulk orders, special promotions and premiums. For details, call Mark Beal at +1.848.992.0391 or email markbeal@markbealmedia.com

DEDICATION

To my wife, Michele, for her selfless support of all my passion projects including this book and for inspiring me to take the first major step in my own transition from a 30-year career in marketing to a new career in academia as a Rutgers University professor.

- Mark Beal

To my wife, Laurie, daughter Julianna and German Shepherd Minnie and my parents and in-laws who are kind enough to share me with those I have helped now for 18+ years. Also, the countless volunteers and speakers that help make The Breakfast Club NJ successful!

- Frank Kovacs

ACKNOWLEDGEMENTS

In 2001, The Breakfast Club NJ (http://www.thebreakfastclubnj. com) was founded by Frank Kovacs to assist individuals in the New York-New Jersey region who were unemployed following the attacks on the United States on September 11, 2001.

We first want to thank The Breakfast Club NJ and other career support networking groups across the United States including, but not limited to, the Professional Services Group (PSG) of Mercer County, Career Support Group at St. Gregory the Great, Professional Service Group of Central New Jersey (PSGCNJ), Monmouth County Division of Workforce Development, and the Philadelphia Area Great Careers Group who are on the front line proactively assisting and supporting individuals who are unemployed and seeking their next opportunity.

We want to thank the thousands of individuals who attend career support networking group meetings like The Breakfast Club NJ. It is your unique career transition journey and proactive mindset to networking and participating in career support group meetings that inspired this book.

We want to thank so many of The Breakfast Club NJ speakers and alums who regularly network and give back in many ways including leading their own career and networking groups including, but not limited to, Benny Recine (St. Gregory The Great), David Schuchman (Professional Services Group Mercer County), Pat Sampson and John Sampson (MIS Networking/Careers In Transition), Gerry Peyton (Project Management Institute, New Jersey Chapter), Brian Mecca (Comp TIA Association of Information Technology Professionals, Garden State Chapter), Ed Pospesil (Technology Executive Network Group), Alex Freund (Barnes & Nobel Networking Group), Janelle Razzino (Hillsdale Career Resource Network), Paul Licata, James Laverty and Robert Skuba (Lehigh Valley Professionals), John Fugazie (Neighbors Helping Neighbors), Maria Heidkamp (Heldrich Center For Workforce Development, Rutgers University), Rod Colon (Own Your Career), Mary Usher (Professional Services Group Central New Jersey), Lynne Williams (Philadelphia Area Great Careers Group) and Christine Dykeman (Monmouth County Division of Workforce Development).

We want to thank Greg Dubas, an executive recruiter, who not only reviewed the original draft of this book and offered his constructive feedback, but for also writing the foreword to the book, leveraging his many years of reviewing resumes, preparing candidates for job interviews and successfully placing individuals into the next job in their career.

We want to thank all the individuals who took quality time to review the early drafts of this book and offered their recommendations and insights including, but not limited to, William Benz, John Brody, PJ Brovak, Paul Capelli, Jerry Clifford, Keith Green, Joe Konopka, Martin Latman, Chris O'Neill, Stan Phelps, Jim Sias, Adrienne Roman, David Siroty, Tom Waldron and many, many more.

We want to thank Evan Carroll for taking our content and transforming it into this published book. Thank you for the time and expertise you dedicated to the layout and design of this book.

Finally, we want to thank all the "givers" in the world. These "givers" are individuals who share their time, support, assistance, counsel and experience to those who are in a career transition and never expect anything in return. It is the "givers" in the world who help those who are unemployed convert opportunities into their next job.

PRAISE FOR
CAREER IN TRANSITION: 101 LESSONS TO ACHIEVE JOB SEARCH SUCCESS

"*Career In Transition: 101 Lessons To Achieve Job Search Success* shares vital and relevant lessons for all of us. From C-Level to just starting on the journey, one should look at every day like an opportunity to take a step on the ladder. All of us should consider our career in a series of phases and we all have ups and downs. Listen to the teachings shared in the book and take a nugget from all of them. We are on this voyage and it is vital to think of it as such. I enjoyed learning and refreshing my thoughts with this helpful read."

JOHN BRODY, SENIOR SPORTS & ENTERTAINMENT MARKETER

"*Career In Transition: 101 Lessons To Achieve Job Search Success* is a great compilation of the steps needed to research, activate and complete your job search. You can look at any of the 101 lessons and increase your rate of success in finding a new position in today's complex job market."

MARTIN LATMAN, ACCOMPLISHED CAREER CFO &
EXECUTIVE DIRECTOR, LATMAN ADVISORY SERVICES LLC

"Finding a job in today's marketplace can be a daunting task and *Career In Transition: 101 Lessons To Achieve Job Search Success* provides the key lessons that can help you gain traction earlier in the search. This is the most comprehensive guide that I have ever seen that enables you to learn from other's lessons rather than having to learn them the hard way."

GERRY PEYTON, AGILE PROJECT MANAGEMENT, PRUDENTIAL FINANCIAL

"*Career In Transition: 101 Lessons To Achieve Job Search Success* should be considered the comprehensive 'career handbook' for both employees that are in transition, and those that are employed. It is an iterative process which helps you to fine-tune your employment journey over your career lifetime. It will become a permanent career reference book in your library. Lots of great advice and practices that will become second nature, if done right!"

ADRIENNE ROMAN, IN TRANSITION - BUT NOT FOR LONG

TABLE OF CONTENTS

PART I: ESTABLISH AND MAINTAIN A POSITIVE MINDSET, ATTITUDE AND OUTLOOK

PART II: TAKE PROACTIVE ACTION TO DRIVE POSITIVE MOMENTUM AND RESULTS

PART III: THINK AND ACT STRATEGICALLY TO ACHIEVE SUCCESS

PART IV: MAKE MAJOR ADVANCES WITH MARKETING, RESEARCH AND PREPARATION

PART V: CONTINUE TO NETWORK, PREPARE AND GIVE BACK

FOREWORD

BY GREG DUBAS

As a veteran executive recruiter who has counseled, guided and placed hundreds of mid, senior and executive level professionals in jobs in the communications and marketing industry, this book, *Career In Transition: 101 Lessons To Achieve Job Search Success*, was not only refreshing to read, but it was on-target and an eye opener.

Whether you are a senior level executive with years of real-world work experience or graduating college with minimal experience just starting your career, *Career In Transition: 101 Lessons To Achieve Job Search Success* is a must read.

In my profession, I find myself frequently engaged in discussions with executives at a point in their careers where they are looking to make a transition and are uncertain how to do so. This book offers a very comprehensive and systematic approach to successfully make that critical career transition.

When it comes to someone just starting their career journey, I would consider this book an invaluable tool. Mark Beal and Frank Kovacs have condensed a very difficult and important journey into easy and manageable "bites" containing "golden nuggets" of information on each page. Reading this book is effortless and allows the reader the ability to absorb the information.

A good deal of *Career In Transition: 101 Lessons To Achieve Job Search Success* is dedicated to technology and social media, which to some senior executives can be intimidating, unfamiliar and frustrating. That said, the authors underscore the critical importance of digital and social media as valuable tools that must be embraced, learned and utilized. Beyond that, they lay out simple approaches to help make technology less daunting.

On the flip side, there is a significant amount of information dedicated to more traditional lessons - hard people skills, personal networking, cup-of-coffee meetings and a "face to face" approach that to the younger generation can be equally as unfamiliar and intimidating. This book really breaks down the approach and helps an individual take the necessary steps to enter these uncharted waters.

As you read *Career In Transition: 101 Lessons To Achieve Job Search Success*, you will find yourself pulled in, often thinking that, "I need to start doing this" or that some of the lessons seem so basic in nature, yet so important. Examples would be doing your research, adapting to the change you seek or learning from your losses or missed opportunities.

If you simply take the time to read, absorb and implement the strategies in, *Career In Transition: 101 Lessons To Achieve Job Search Success* it will put you in the driver's seat of your career and destiny. This book is adaptable for a professional at any stage in their career and there is no expiration date for the lessons enclosed.

INTRODUCTION

In early 2019, I was invited to deliver a speech at 8:00 a.m. on a cold and damp winter Saturday in East Brunswick, New Jersey to a group called The Breakfast Club NJ. I did not know much about the organization other than that it was a career support networking group where individuals who were in a career transition and seeking their next job opportunity came to collaborate and gain helpful advice and counsel.

Two years earlier, after I had authored and published *101 Lessons They Never Taught You In College*, I started receiving invitations from career support networking groups throughout New Jersey and Pennsylvania to deliver speeches regarding how job seekers could market themselves as they competed for opportunities. While my first book was intended to help college students prepare for their transition from college to a career, many of the lessons were applicable to people in their 30s, 40s, 50s and 60s who were out of work and competing to rejoin the workforce.

Prior to speaking to The Breakfast Club NJ, I had delivered speeches to approximately 10 other career support group meetings. The crowds ranged from as small as 25 to as many as 100 and the venues varied from old church basements to state-of-the art libraries. Each and every time after I spoke to a career support group, I was more inspired by the individuals who were out-of-work than I ever could have imagined.

That was no different on the day I presented to more than 80 job seekers who attended The Breakfast Club NJ meeting. It was also that same day when I met Frank Kovacs who founded The Breakfast Club NJ after the attacks of September 11, 2001 to help so many residents of the New York-New Jersey area who were out of work and unemployed. Since 2001, Frank and The Breakfast Club NJ have helped thousands of individuals secure their next job after experiencing unemployment.

While presenting to The Breakfast Club NJ, I experienced something that I had never experienced prior. The organizer of the group, Frank Kovacs, was providing color commentary like Tony Romo in the CBS broadcast booth during the national telecast of a Sunday NFL game. Frank and I didn't rehearse, and actually, we didn't even speak prior to my presentation, but as the founder of the group, it was Frank's floor and he felt empowered to share his commentary as I delivered my slides. I did not take offense. I actually enjoyed the way we spontaneously played off each other's advice to the audience. I soon realized that I was delivering recommendations to the job seekers from a marketing perspective and Frank was delivering sound technical advice and the two complemented each other incredibly well for the benefit of all the attendees.

As I drove away from that Saturday morning meeting south on Route 18, I was inspired again by all the job seekers and their stories, but this time, I was inspired enough to start writing this book. Less than 24 hours later, I received a LinkedIn message from Frank also proposing that we write this book. Unbeknown to Frank, I had the exact same idea and after 48 hours of emailing each other back and forth, we were off to the races writing this book with the sole mission to help as many people as we could who were unemployed.

This book is intended to be a helpful resource for anyone who is seeking their next job no matter their age or the circumstance for their unemployment. The book sources job seeking experts as well as testimonials from individuals who experienced their own career transition in the past 24 months. It also features all the knowledge and wisdom that Frank has accumulated in leading The Breakfast Club NJ over the past two decades including his incredible strategic approach as well his technical insights coupled with my point-of-view on marketing your personal brand.

Frank and I hope that these 101 lessons inspire, motivate and energize you as you experience your own unique career transition journey. Most importantly, we hope that it helps lead you to secure your next opportunity and begin the next chapter in your career. Best wishes for great success on your journey.

PART I

ESTABLISH AND MAINTAIN A POSITIVE MINDSET, ATTITUDE AND OUTLOOK

LESSON 1

YOUR JOURNEY IS UNIQUE

While millions of people have experienced a transition in their professional career, whether forced or on their own terms, the first, and perhaps most important lesson, is that no two career transition journeys are the same. While we can learn extensive lessons and insights from those who have made a successful transition in their careers, each and every one of us takes our own journey based on our industry, past professional experience, education, members of our professional network, past clients, customers and colleagues, family, salary level, geographic location, lifestage, money saved and invested, and future goals, objectives, dreams and ambitions. In other words, this is your one and only employment journey. The Minnesota State Colleges and Universities Careerwise digital hub summarized it well when they wrote, "Think of your career journey as climbing a ladder. Each step of the ladder could be a job that gives you a unique experience. At one job, you might pick up new skills. At another, you might gain a new interest. In all of your jobs, you'll collect valuable experiences."[1] Because this is your unique career journey, you get to make the rules and navigate the ship. You get to determine how much sweat equity you want to invest or how many cup-of-coffee meetings you want to schedule. Most importantly, you get to author your own career transition playbook in the same way that NFL head coaches do before the game on Sunday. There is no right or wrong way to take your journey just like there is no right or wrong way to hike a mountain. There may be paths you will take that will prove to be more efficient, productive or easier to navigate, but that is part of the testing and learning

---

1. https://careerwise.minnstate.edu/careers/journey.html

you will do along your journey to the next destination in your professional career. Embrace and enjoy this unique journey as it is the only one that will ever exist, and along the way, evolve and transform as you prepare to write the next chapter in your career.

LESSON 2

CHANGE IS GOOD

Robin Sharma, one of the world's top leadership experts and author of The Greatness Guide: 101 Lessons For Making What's Good At Work And Life Even Better, said, "Change is hard at first, messy in the middle and gorgeous at the end." Simply translated, change is good. Perhaps there is no better way to describe a transition in your career and the changes it brings to you, your family, friends and your way of living than Sharma's quote. However, once you battle through the hard part and muddle through the messy phase, your next act will be beautiful, fulfilling and rewarding. As we each get older and further along in our career, it is natural for all of us to settle into routines. From the time we wake up to the time we leave for work each day, our life becomes a series of regular routines. Routines feel comfortable and safe, but they also lull us to sleep so when a drastic change like a reduction in force or a forced retirement arrives at our workplace, it is "hard" as Sharma describes. Instead of fighting change, embrace it. Change will force you out of your routines and out of your comfort zone. That is a great thing. Change in your career will motivate you to reconnect with individuals in your network, dust off your resume and take inventory of your past, present and future. Change will also result in you meeting new people and making new connections. Change will challenge you strategically and creatively. Change will inspire you to learn and evolve so much more than if you kept your existing job and your existing routines for the next several years. Change is not only good. Change is great! Embrace change and be energized by it. Change will ultimately not only help you successfully make a career transition, but it will empower you to transform professionally and personally.

LESSON 3

99 PERCENT OF PEOPLE ARE GIVERS

As you go through your transition, you must believe and be confident that the overwhelmingly majority of people in your professional and personal networks are "givers" and they want to help you on your journey. Even people you don't know yet, but who you will meet on your journey, will want to "give" and help you. Adam Grant, an organizational psychologist who authored, *Give and Take: A Revolutionary Approach To Success*, agrees that most successful leaders are givers. In an interview with Inc., he said, "First, it's easier for leaders to multiply themselves and create networks of givers. To build cultures where that's the norm and, as a result, to be able to delegate a lot of the giving to people around and below them. That provides an opportunity to spread their giving farther than people who are not at the top." In his quote, Grant captures the essence of the network of giving that you need to immerse yourself in and leverage as you search for your next act. However, you need to arm all your givers, both leaders and those delegates who comprise their network of givers, with the right assets and ammunition to effectively assist you. Just because most people want to give does not mean they can do it on their own. They need the pieces to the puzzle that are going to make a connection to your next opportunity. In other words, you need to proactively communicate with them consistently and provide valuable information. If they are going to make an investment in giving to your career transition journey, you need to make an even greater investment in clearly identifying industries and organizations you are prospecting and the names of individuals you are trying to secure an audience with. In other words, make it as easy as possible for the "givers" to give. [2]

---

2. https://www.inc.com/leigh-buchanan/adam-grant-leadership-give-and-take.html

LESSON 4

PERFECT YOUR PUZZLE

At the Saturday morning Breakfast Club NJ career networking meeting in East Brunswick, New Jersey where individuals in career transition meet to collaborate, network and support each other, an executive who was recently employed returned to the meeting to deliver his message that succeeding in a career transition is like trying to complete a one-of-a-kind jigsaw puzzle. Jo Green, a Career Change Coach, reinforced that notion in a column she wrote titled, "Why Changing Your Career Is A Lot Like Doing A Jigsaw Puzzle." As she reminisced about her own career transition, Green wrote, "I recognized the need to see the small things come together, much like doing a big jigsaw puzzle. I needed to practice the twin arts of patience and pattern spotting. These are the same skills we use to piece together a jigsaw puzzle. Turning a mound of disconnected fragments into a satisfyingly complete and complex image takes time and tenacity. It also takes imagination and intuition. It's absorbing and frustrating and fun." If you can take the approach that your transition to the next opportunity in your career is like completing your own jigsaw puzzle, it will put you in the right mindset to manage, as Green describes, the frustrating and fun phases of your journey. Your puzzle pieces are the individuals in your network and those who you will meet along the way who will help you connect and complete your puzzle. The pieces are also a variety of puzzle-solving moments where you are inspired by others as well as the research you conduct, and right before your eyes, you will witness your puzzle starting to take shape. There will be frustrating days when you don't complete one piece of the puzzle and fun days when you complete entire sections. Either way, stay focused, positive and confident in solving your puzzle because once you do, you will have successfully secured your next opportunity.[3]

---

3. https://collectivehub.com/2017/08/why-changing-career-is-a-lot-like-doing-a-jigsaw-puzzle/

LESSON 5

PURSUE YOUR PASSION

Billionaire Mark Cuban, owner of the NBA's Dallas Mavericks, proclaimed, "One of the great lies of life is 'follow your passions,'" as part of the Amazon Insights for Entrepreneurs series. Mr. Cuban, we respectfully disagree with you especially when it comes to a career transition. There are a million stories of individuals who not only successfully followed their passion, but also converted their passion into a successful business as their second act. Perhaps, that passion did not translate into billions of dollars, but not everyone like you needs to earn a billion dollars to be successful and happy. Take Tom Waldron, a New Jersey State Trooper who retired at the age of 50 and then took his passion for fitness and exercise and transformed that passion into a personal training business that is now more than a decade into existence and can boast of hundreds if not thousands of happy clients. Tom could have sought and settled for a typical security job, but instead, he and his entrepreneurial spirit pursued his passion and the second act of his career led to him becoming the CEO of his own company, a company he was passionate about when he started it and is even more passionate about now more than a decade later. Tom commented, "I encourage anyone who is embarking on a second career to focus on an activity that they have a passion for and try to find a way to monetize it. The energy you bring to this new beginning will be off the charts which will maximize your chance for success." As you set off on your career transition journey, take quality time to map out all your passions – music, fashion, sports, education, travel, pets, classic cars, even fitness – and consider how you might convert that passion into your next act either as an employee of a company that specializes in that passion or, like Tom, the state police officer, as your own start-up company. There was never a law passed that regulated that you could not have fun at work. Instead, live by the famous quote, "Choose a job you love, and you will never have to work a day in your life." In order to accomplish that, your next act in your career must be one where you are applying your craft to something you are incredibly passionate about. [4]

4. https://www.cnbc.com/2018/02/16/mark-cuban-follow-your-passion-is-bad-advice.html

LESSON 6

IT WILL TAKE A VILLAGE

Family, friends (old and new), neighbors, college classmates, past colleagues, professional and personal contacts, the barista at your favorite coffee shop and even the bartender at your favorite tavern - each and every one could potentially play a role in helping you secure the next opportunity in your career. It will take a village to land your next job. In an article about the New Start Career Network in New Jersey, a journalist wrote that the organization, "is taking an innovative approach to ending unemployment by developing a village of volunteer coaches who are helping job seekers ages 45 and older, learn and apply practical job search techniques, and by offering hope and inspiration." Do not proceed one day thinking you will do it on your own. Put aside your pride and your ego. Equally important, keep your eyes and ears wide open each and every day throughout your transition. "I've been in several job searches and after being downsized at the age of 53, I started my own business," commented David Siroty, a senior public relations and marketing executive. "At every step, I relied on so many people to help me. And each time, I found that it was people I wasn't expecting who not only jumped into help, but who would stay in contact offering a kind word and getting me through a disruption. The networks we've built have to be used. There are a ton of amazing people in our lives." Perfect strangers may hold the key to unlocking the door to your next opportunity. The more proactive you are in your approach and the more time you invest in networking and scheduling meetings, not only will your village expand, but so will the number of opportunities. Ultimately, you will secure that next job, but it will most likely occur because of someone you knew who knew someone who knew someone who knew someone who knew someone who opened a door that you busted wide open![5]

5. https://www.mycentraljersey.com/story/money/business/2016/07/03/
imagine-takes-village-help-long-term-unemployed/86569048/

LESSON 7

SUCCESS IS A MARATHON

While most individuals who find themselves searching for their next job, come out of the blocks like a sprinter thinking they will be back at work in the next month or two, it is better to start your journey with the mindset and mental toughness of a marathoner because you are most likely in the running for a longer race than you expected and along the way, just like a marathoner, you are going to need to slow down to refuel and pace yourself so that you can successfully cross the finish line. A senior marketing communications executive commented, "Preparing yourself for a longer journey will help minimize the emotional valleys when disappointments come along. You're in it for the long haul and your mind should reflect that." In an article titled, "The Job Search is a Marathon, not a Sprint – Treat it as such," the reporter writes, "All too often, a day feels like a week and a week can feel like a month – particularly for those who haven't had to look for a job in years." Your marathon is going to consist of thousands of phone calls, texts and emails with the allies in your network. It's also going to feature the submission and completion of many applications as well as a series of informal and formal interviews by Skype, phone, one-on-one, panels and even committees. If it was easy, everyone who is out of work would be right back at a new job. However, it is not easy. It is painful - physically, mentally and emotionally. It can play tricks with your mind and psyche like miles 20 through 26 in a marathon. If you can start and continue your journey with the mindset that you are going to run a marathon for the next six to 12 months and each day is another mile on your journey, your unique finish line will come into focus on your own time based on the path you have taken.[6]

6. https://www.careerattraction.com/marathon/

LESSON 8

SWALLOW YOUR PRIDE

There is no room for pride when you are experiencing a transition in your career, especially an unexpected transition. In other words, don't be so proud that you are afraid to share the news that you were laid off or your company had a reduction in force. Keith Green said, "As a public relations and marketing communications professional, it might seem odd that I had a hard time with this during my transition. And that probably was a mistake. My reasons were numerous, including being unsure of exactly what I wanted to do next, which made it more difficult to clearly and succinctly share with people in my network what I was after. And if that is the case with you, then I would recommend having the confidence to share that your answer could be different to different people depending upon the role you are seeking and the type of industry job you are chasing." Don't be so proud that you don't ask for help, support and assistance from those allies in your network. Don't be so proud that you won't attend a career support networking group meeting. Don't be so proud that you don't share thought leadership or content about your unique career transition on your social and professional channels. Don't be so proud that you don't seek out and schedule informal cup-of-coffee meetings to ask questions and learn. Don't be so proud that you don't mobilize your contacts when you formally apply for a job. Don't be so proud that you don't learn from rejection. In an article titled, "5 Reasons You Should Swallow Your Pride and Ask for Feedback After Getting Rejected," Kat Boogaard writes, "Getting rejected is never fun. And, asking for input and advice afterward can undoubtedly be a little awkward. But, that doesn't change the fact that it's the perfect opportunity to gain some useful insight into ways you can better yourself—and your job hunt! So, swallow your pride and hit 'reply' on that dreaded rejection email." No matter the circumstances that have you seeking your next career opportunity, put your pride aside during the transition and pick it up again when you secure that new job and you are back to work.[7]

---

7. https://www.themuse.com/advice/5-reasons-you-should-swallow-your-pride-and-ask-for-feedback-after-getting-rejected

LESSON 9

ANYONE CAN OPEN THE DOOR TO YOUR NEXT OPPORTUNITY

In an article titled, "How To Convince Strangers To Help You Get A Job," Alex Lacey writes, "In my recent job search, I received referrals for 40 jobs at 40 hard-to-reach companies despite not knowing anyone at 38 of them." Lacey used strangers who he proactively introduced himself to on LinkedIn to help him secure his next job. As you transition, consistently keep an open mind with regard to meeting new people and the role they will potentially play in your journey.

"You never know where that job lead will come. I found my first corporate job out of college while waiting tables. A regular customer worked at a public relations firm and offered me a job solely based on the interactions we had at the restaurant," recalled a public relations veteran. Another executive commented, "Sometimes you just never really know who knows who. One of your friends or colleagues might have attended college with someone who can get you visibility with your next job destination of choice." When and where you least expect it, one meeting, one phone call, one email or one chance encounter with a total stranger could be the connection to your next opportunity. Each day when you wake, set out on your day with the objective to meet and network with as many new people as possible. Each person you meet will help you complete the jigsaw puzzle that is your journey to the next opportunity in your career.[8]

---

8. https://www.freecodecamp.org/news/how-to-convince-strangers-to-help-you-get-a-job-35db34549ac4/

LESSON 10

OWN YOUR JOURNEY

❝ We aspire to a higher level of human achievement. The power to create and become who we want is in our minds and in our hands. We design our journey and the life we are called to live." Christopher Connors penned those inspiring words in a column he wrote about the journey to a job titled, "You Design Your Journey – Not Your Job." You are the owner, operator and CEO of your journey that is the transition to your next career opportunity so own every aspect of it. As you transition, own the setbacks. If you look to others to take ownership, you are giving up control of your journey. Yes, you will have an army of allies who will be eager to lend their assistance and support, but you need to own every one of those relationships and every step and meeting that you take with them. You are the only one who can take ownership of your unique journey each and every day. As the CEO of your one and only career transition journey, you will have deputies and partners, but you will need to own the go-to-market campaign and set the strategy as well as the executional tactics.[9]

---

9. https://medium.com/@chrisdconnors/you-design-your-journey-not-your-job-89a26ded8ca8

LESSON 11

THERE WILL BE GOOD DAYS AND BAD DAYS

"Job searching is hard. It's hard for most people – for me, for you, for your friend's cousin," wrote Alyse Kalish in an article titled, "How To Pull Yourself Through A Rough Job Search When You Feel Like Giving Up." Until that day when you win the recruiting and selection process and are offered a formal employment contract, you will most likely have more bad days than good days on your way to the next opportunity in your career. Every job rejection or remark that you are overqualified or last-minute cancellation of an important networking meeting will contribute to a negative attitude and mindset. "There will very dark days that will lead you to question yourself, regardless of the reason for leaving your previous job," said Keith Green, a marketing and public relations practitioner. "You will go on an emotional roller coaster picturing yourself in new and potentially exciting roles as opportunities arise. And if you are looking at jobs that would require you to move, the mental part of that is also difficult. The level of uncertainty can get you down, but fight through it because something better is coming next." Learn lessons from the setbacks and failures and quickly proceed ahead on a positive path. You want to start to recall all the small victories that you have had on your journey that put you in a position for an opportunity to be a finalist or that helped you secure an audience with key decision makers. Positivity is contagious and infectious. By being positive in everything you do - posting content, participating in career transition meetings and proactively networking - you will engage and mobilize your followers in a way that will create a positive movement on your behalf that will lead to the ultimate victory, the next opportunity in your career.[10]

10. https://www.themuse.com/advice/how-to-pull-yourself-through-a-rough-job-search-when-you-feel-like-giving-up

LESSON 12

STAY THE COURSE

"Whatever course you decide upon, there is always someone to tell you that you are wrong. There are always difficulties arising which tempt you to believe that your critics are right. To map out a course of action and follow it to an end requires courage." Ralph Waldo Emerson

Throughout your transition to your next career opportunity, there are going to be many starts, stops and even detours. There will probably even be a few exit ramps. No matter what, stay the course. In other words, as you take your unique career transition journey and learn from the wins and the losses, as well as the advice and counsel from a wide variety of individuals and sources, including the critics and naysayers, continue to stay the course towards your ultimate objective – securing that new job opportunity that you have been strategically targeting and prospecting. A senior marketer said, "Whenever possible, stay clear of naysayers. If someone says, 'who are you to think you can achieve success.' Remind them 'who am I to think that I can't.'" You have to continuously remind yourself that this is your unique journey. You are the map maker and the navigator. You will have first mates and second mates along the way, but as the captain, it is all up to you to stay the course to your ultimate destination.

LESSON 13

BE POSITIVE

"Once you replace negative thoughts with positive ones, you'll start having positive results." Willie Nelson

You have every right to have a negative mindset. After all, you are out-of-work and you may not have any solid job prospects on the immediate horizon. However, if you start from a place of negativity, it is also going to spread throughout your entire network. Instead, your positivity and a positive approach to your job search and prospecting will effectively rally others to mobilize and support your cause. "It is easy to dwell on the negative aspects of losing a job," commented a brand marketing veteran. "For the first six weeks after I was let go, it was hard for me to reconcile why I hadn't heard from certain people I worked with. I was as pleasantly surprised by the people I heard from as I was disappointed in the ones who hadn't reached out. Someone you might have said hello to and worked closely with for a period of time isn't necessarily your friend. Remember, it's business and it's transactional, so don't let it bother you or eat you up." When you exude a positive outlook, energy and vibes, you inspire those who are in your network to go the extra mile on your behalf and you motivate new contacts to you join your network and your cause. Of course, there are going to be negative moments and experiences, but learn from them, shrug them off and proceed down the highway to positivity because it is that path that is going to deliver positive results and bring you closer to your next career opportunity

LESSON 14

SURROUND YOURSELF WITH SUPPORTERS

World traveler, adventure and author Leon Logothetis wrote, "When you're surrounded by good people, you're surrounded by life. You'll be less stressed and find more joy in daily things. Today, make a commitment to start spending more time with the good people in your life." Leon was writing about surrounding yourself with good people and supporters in life, not your job search, but the same principle applies to your career transition. There is no room on your journey for negativity. There is no room for people on the ship you are captaining who use the word, "can't" in their vocabulary. As you embark on your unique journey, you are going to quickly learn which individuals in your personal and professional network are going to rally to support your cause and those who are just giving you lip service and don't have enough concern or interest to invest their time or effort. "My wife was tremendous during my transition. She knew exactly when I needed support and to talk, and when to give me my space. There's a bit of an art form to that, and she was incredibly helpful through the highs and lows," commented Keith Green, a marketing and communications professional.

Align yourself with all of those individuals who show genuine support and will deliver value in the form of assistance. When it comes to your supporters, it will be a case of quality over quantity. Ten quality supporters will deliver greater value, counsel and positive mojo to you than 100 acquaintances. Surround yourself each and every day with your true supporters. [11]

11. https://www.huffpost.com/entry/kkeeping-good-company-why-you-should-surround-yourself-with-good-people_b_6816468

LESSON 15

PERSEVERANCE CREATES OPPORTUNITIES

❝Gallup published results of a poll in 2011 suggesting that millions of unemployed job seekers, as much as 14 million at that time, felt demoralized, unmotivated and lacked the energy to find a new job. Yet, many people eventually find employment, and it is partly based on persevering throughout the phases of the job search process." By definition, according to Webster's Dictionary, perseverance means the continued effort to do or achieve something despite difficulties, failure, or opposition. If that doesn't sound like searching for a job in the midst of a career transition, nothing does. Each and every day of your job search, there will be hurdles, roadblocks, rejection and failure. You have two choices. You could give in to the setbacks and determine that you will never work again. However, we all know that is not true. So, instead of delaying the inevitable of securing that next job opportunity, push through the obstacles immediately and demonstrate a high degree of perseverance and persistence. If you can demonstrate these admirable qualities, it will positively mobilize your personal and professional network while helping you secure your next opportunity sooner. [12]

---

12. https://work.chron.com/perseverance-helps-job-6219.html

LESSON 16

CREATE YOUR OWN DESTINY

In a column titled, "7 Tips For Creating Your Own Destiny," Kevin Daum writes, "Too many people whine about not having the life they want. The main reason people fall short of their own expectations is the same reason most companies fail to achieve their objectives: poor planning and execution." Throughout this book, we have emphasized that the career transition that you are experiencing now is your own unique journey. Well, the same can be said about creating your own destiny. There are no rules regulating how you go about creating your next job opportunity. It's one of the reasons we wrote this book so that you could apply as many or as few of these 101 recommendations to your journey so that you could create your own destiny. You should seek guidance, counsel, recommendations, tips and lessons like those featured in this book, but you and you alone will create your own destiny and your own path to your future job and career. Today, you may have no idea where that destiny will take you, but everything you invest – research, referrals and reunions with former colleagues and classmates – will empower you to create your own destiny. A destiny that you will turn around and share with others in need once you have secured your next opportunity.[13]

---

13. https://www.inc.com/kevin-daum/7-tips-for-creating-your-own-destiny.html

LESSON 17

LEARNING IS A JOURNEY

It's only after we graduate college and we begin our careers that the real learning begins. For many years, you have learned on the job. Well now, you are going to learn so much more off the job. You are going to learn more about human relations than ever before. You are going to learn what motivates individuals in your network to act on your behalf. You are going to learn how challenging it is to strategically navigate your way into a corner office meeting at one of the organizations you have been targeting and prospecting. Embrace and celebrate everything you are learning. Consider this career transition the greatest final exam you will ever take in your life, but you already know you are going to earn an "A" because one day, all of your preparation and studying and learning is going to pay off. Learning is a journey and this career transition journey will take you to your ultimate destination, but take time each day to enjoy each step of your journey and the learnings along the way.

LESSON 18

LEARN FROM THE LOSSES

Henry Ford stated, "Failure is simply the opportunity to begin again, this time more intelligently." In a career transition, you are going to experience failure at least once or you would not be in a transitional phase. The most important thing you can do is to learn from each failure and approach the next opportunity as intelligently as Ford emphasizes. Each time you interview for a job and don't get it, ask for the reasons why. Whether you were eliminated from contention after your first interview or advanced all the way to the final round, ask the recruiter for specific reasons why someone was selected over you. Typically, you will receive a response like, "It was a very difficult decision and you finished a very close second." While they may be trying to be kind in giving you that type of response, that doesn't help you at all. Instead ask by saying, "As I interview for other jobs, I would love to learn from this process. Can you provide me some constructive criticism that I can learn from and apply to my next opportunity?" In exchange for the investment in time and resources that you made for a job application and interview process that could have taken weeks if not months, you have to take away key lessons and learnings and immediately apply those to the next opportunity. There is no greater waste of time and effort than not learning valuable lessons from the losses and failures.

LESSON 19

EXPERIENCE IS EARNED

Yoga teacher and author Stephanie Spence said, "Experience is earned, not randomly gained. Wisdom is given to those who work for it. If it was easy to grow everyone would do it." Stephanie's "Experience is earned," quote is as applicable to your career transition journey as any other quote. As you advance on your unique journey, you will be earning valuable experience with every meeting, interview and proactive participation in a career networking support group or industry meetup. With those experiences will come wisdom that should fuel your next set of strategic moves. You are not only working to earn that wisdom, but you are also working to apply it to the individuals and companies you are targeting and prospecting. As Spence concludes, "If it was easy to grow, everyone would do it." Celebrate that you are growing each and every day. Celebrate that the experienced earned, the wisdom gained and your growth and transformation is leading you in a positive direction to the next opportunity in your career.

LESSON 20

DON'T FORGET KARMA

Whether you call it destiny or fate, just like the "favor bank" we feature later in this book, positive karma can always come back in your favor when you least expect it or you need it the most. Each and every day, continue to share positive energy and vibes and your network will rally around that positivity. Even as you seek help, continue to assist others in need. While your greatest priority will be to secure that next career opportunity, someone in your network may call you out of the blue to help their son or daughter get an internship with a company you have a relationship with. Yes, it will take you a few minutes away from your focus, but your investment in time and resources to help someone else will only help you somewhere down the road. That's why you never forget karma, especially positive karma.

LESSON 21

LEAVE THE PAST BEHIND AND CREATE A FUTURE VISION

We just had this conversation with two friends we were networking with over breakfast. Your LinkedIn profile and resume are not your life's biography or obituary. This career transition journey is not about where you've been. It's about where you are going and what you want to do. Flip the bit and think of this from the employer's point-of-view. The work environment and the needs of employers are changing rapidly due to the digital revolution. Employers need employees with strong competencies to help their firm meet this challenge. Therefore, jettison those things that are painting you as a "legacy" resource and identify those things that are consistent with presenting you as a candidate that you have the skills and competencies that they need to fulfill their strategic goals and achieve success. As you go through your resume and LinkedIn profile ensure that you carefully select PARs (Problem Action Result, refer to Lesson 56) and word them in such a way that they convey an image of you that matches the employer's needs - never put anything false down, but always write within the constraints of your actual experience and capabilities. You need to do the same thing on your LinkedIn profile by carefully selecting those skills that are in high demand that you possess. This also applies to your professional references so that they include verbiage in their recommendation that highlights your skills and experience consistent with the opportunities you are pursuing.

LESSON 22

MASTER THE SIX DEGREES OF YOUR JOB SEARCH

The world we live in is all driven by six degrees of separation. We are all connected. In your job search, it is all about maximizing and leveraging those connections to deliver success. So, grow and nurture your contacts and your network so that you evolve them into relationships that you can tap into to maximize the benefit that your network can deliver for you. "Cultivate your contacts by offering them something of value, when they don't expect it," says Paul Capelli, whose 30-year career includes communications leadership positions at Fortune 500 companies, leading media organizations and top-ranked agencies. "It need be only a simple bit of information or thought that shows you are thinking of others best interests -- everyone likes a heads-up on a new idea; an emerging trend; a new source of information online, etc." Focus and set a specific time each week that you invest in growing your contacts and strengthening the relationships with those in your network both during the job search, at the firm where you land your next job, and throughout your career once you are back working. So many individuals succumb to the pitfall that they don't have the time to continue networking proactively, but with digital disruption impacting businesses, many workers are finding themselves in transition more than once in their career. Therefore, it is critical to stay connected and continuously be working to grow and strengthen your network. Your success will be helped greatly by making the six degrees of separation work for you. Capelli adds, "When the time comes, it's much easier to ask of your network for a referral, job lead or recommendation, knowing you have established yourself as a 'giver' not just a connection that reaches out in times of need."

PART 2

TAKE ACTION TO DRIVE POSITIVE MOMENTUM AND RESULTS

LESSON 23

BE PROACTIVE

In a column titled, "5 Ways To Stop Feeling Helpless and Start Taking the Job Hunt Into Your Own Hands," Lily Zhang writes, "One thing that's important to acknowledge is how critical it is to stay motivated. Sending in your materials to one job and then waiting around with fingers crossed won't do that for you. You need to stay driven in order to keep the ball in your court." If you take only one lesson away from this book, this is the one, be proactive in everything you do throughout your transition. A reactive or passive approach to prospecting for your next job opportunity will get you nowhere. From setting your alarm in the morning to getting a jumpstart on the day's agenda to making a conscious effort each day to expand your network, don't sit around waiting for the phone to ring or for an organization to respond to a resume you submitted. There will be times when you need to be reactive when opportunity knocks, but the only way opportunity is ever going to knock is as a result of your consistent proactive mindset, approach and execution. Stephen Covey said it best. "People who end up with the good jobs are the proactive ones who are solutions to problems, not problems themselves, who seize the initiative to do whatever is necessary to get the job done." [14]

---

14. https://www.themuse.com/advice/5-ways-to-stop-feeling-helpless-and-start-taking-the-job-hunt-into-your-own-hands

LESSON 24

REV UP YOUR MORNING ROUTINE

"Early to bed and early to rise makes a man healthy, wealthy and wise." Ben Franklin is credited with uttering this famous phrase more than 225 years ago, but it is more relevant today than ever for anyone who is in the midst of a job search. While it is very important to use this transition in your career as a time to break out and disrupt the regular routines that you got used to while you were in your last job, that doesn't mean that you should be sleeping in until 12:00 noon. The one routine that you should maintain... or actually rev up, is setting your alarm clock and waking up early to take on the challenges of the day. If your former routine included rising early and working out before commuting to your job, continue to do so and wake-up even earlier. Getting off to a strong, confident and energizing start each day will provide you positive momentum as you proactively prospect your target companies while reacting to any unexpected opportunities that arrive via phone, email or a LinkedIn message. If you even want to take it one step further, dress for success, and get out of your pajamas and into a suit and tie or at least business casual attire. Whatever helps you best jumpstart each day of your unique journey, just do it. Nobody else is going to do it for you.

LESSON 25

DO SOMETHING FOR THE FIRST TIME

Ask yourself, "When was the last time you did something for the first time?" That question was popular well before Darius Rucker led off his hit song, "For The First Time," with that question in 2017. It is human nature for individuals to get comfortable in their routines as they approach their 30s, 40s, 50s and 60s. Think back to when you were a teenager and all your "firsts" – first job, first paycheck, first car, first time driving, first time moving away from home. All of those "firsts" were about exploring and discovering new people, places and experiences. That is exactly what you need to do now. You need to recapture your teenage zest for discovery and exploration. This is the time to break your routines. After all, you don't have a job to report to by 9:00 a.m. Instead, for the first time in your life, take that bold step and attend your first career networking support group meeting. We can promise you that once you attend your first, you will not only find value and camaraderie, but you will quickly research other similar groups in your region. For the first time, meet one-on-one with a career coach and determine if they can be of assistance. For the first time, ask your former colleagues for assistance and support. You may be hesitant, but the vast majority of them want to help you. They just need your direction. At least once a week throughout your career transition, you should be "doing something for the first time" – and enjoying every minute of it.

LESSON 26

PUT YOURSELF OUT THERE

In a blog post titled, "Putting Yourself Out There: Taking Steps to Land a Job," Danielle Dresden writes, "Getting noticed is the key to getting work of any kind. And these days, with fewer jobs and more ways to promote yourself, simply answering ads and sending in resumes is a sure way to get stuck on the sidelines." No matter the reason that you are in a transition in your career, now is the time to be proactive and vocal even if that has not been your style. As Dresden notes, you need to be an active participant in the career transition game and simply submitting your resume to online job postings is considered standing on the sidelines in today's social and digital media society. Meetups, career networking meetings, mix and mingles – no matter what they call it, if it involves people coming together to network and discuss jobs and careers, you need to attend and be a proactive participant. It also means scheduling one-on-one cup-of-coffee meetings and shaking as many hands as you are able like you are running for office. Whether it is former college classmates, past work colleagues or strangers who you meet at a career transition networking meeting, every person you meet can help you complete the jigsaw puzzle that is your transition to your next opportunity. While for many of us, "putting yourself out there" is uncomfortable and maybe even feel a bit weird, it is a necessary step in your career transition journey. Yes, you can put yourself out there by blogging and tweeting, but you also need to do it the old school way by meeting face-to-face, sharing your brand narrative and asking for assistance. So, start scheduling one-on-one meetings with as many people in your network as you are able to and conduct a simple online search for any meetups in your region whether they are career transition meetings or gatherings that are specifically focused on the industry where you are pursuing your next opportunity. Each meeting you schedule or attend will empower you by expanding your network and learning new insights and information that will inform your next series of moves to that next opportunity.[15]

15. https://workbloom.com/job-search/putting-yourself-out-there-taking-steps-to-land-a-job.aspx

LESSON 27

DUST OFF YOUR ROLODEX

For those who are old enough to know what a Rolodex is, you should easily understand what this lesson means. For those who are not of age, this lesson could simply be called, "Review Your LinkedIn Contacts," or "Scroll Through Your Contacts On Your Phone." You have probably accrued more contacts than you will ever remember, but once a contact, always a contact. The easiest way to manage this process is to simply review all your contacts on LinkedIn alphabetically. Of course, there will be some contacts who you never really had much contact with at all. But, like finding a needle in a haystack, you will start to come across names of people who you collaborated closely with at one time but have just not stayed in touch with. Many of those individuals have gone on to new organizations in senior roles where they most likely can provide assistance especially if you are both still in the same industry. "What I found so humbling to me during my search process was that people who I hadn't worked directly with in more than 15 years were so willing to make introductions and recommend me to those in their networks," remarked PJ Brovak, a marketing communications professional. There is no room for an ego when you are going through a career transition, so put your ego and everything else aside and catch-up with former colleagues and past contacts and learn what doors they may be able to open. The worst thing that could happen is that they don't return your LinkedIn message or your phone call. If that is the case, they probably weren't going to deliver much value to your journey to your next career opportunity.

LESSON 28

RECONNECT WITH FORMER CONTACTS

Former classmates, co-workers, colleagues, neighbors, fellow members of associations and groups that you belonged to are a great way to build, grow and mobilize your network. Previously we spoke of how you can take your email contact list and LinkedIn has an automated way of comparing these contacts identifying matches and automatically requesting that they connect with you on LinkedIn. Going to expos, joining networking groups, attending professional association meetings is a great way to identify potential contacts but it is up to you to put in the effort to establish relationships with these contacts and then maintain those relationships. "A similar tactic is to reconnect with your university. Almost every school will have a career center for students and alums, so take advantage and see what jobs and resources your alma mater has available," commented Keith Green, a longtime marketer who has also taught at several universities. So, plan time both when employed and when not, to focus on growing your contacts, nurturing your relationships, and making your network as strong as you are able. Keith Ferrazzi authored the book, *Who's Got Your Back*, and speaks to how to effectively work with your contacts to ensure you create and nurture strong relationships with those in your network.

LESSON 29

CREATE CONNECTIONS WITH CUP-OF-COFFEE MEETINGS

There is no less intimidating way to secure a meeting with someone you are targeting and prospecting than simply asking if they would like to meet over a cup-of-coffee. In a column that one of the authors of this book, Mark Beal, wrote for Grit Daily, titled, "Hey Gen Z: Good Ol' Human Interaction Is Still Core To Landing Those Entry Level Jobs," Beal writes, "Almost every executive at one of your target companies will take a cup-of-coffee meeting because there's no risk and most people want to give back and help... (those) attempting to break into the business. But for you, the cup-of-coffee meeting is critically important and offers a low risk, high reward opportunity. First, a cup-of-coffee meeting gets you into the building. It gives you an opportunity to see inside your target company. If you execute your cup-of-coffee meeting at a high level, it will allow you to bypass the robotic and tech-centric recruitment process...and enables you to establish a powerful ally on the inside who could get your resume in front of the right recruiter." Forget the steak dinners and two-martini lunches, all it takes is a simple cup-of-coffee to successfully create a connection with someone who can be converted into your advocate as you strategically target a role at an organization where they may have influence. Make it as easy as possible for the individual who you are prospecting with. Identify a café next door to their office or in their hometown. Make it so easy that they can't refuse. Use cup-of-coffee meetings to your advantage as they do not come with the stress and anxiety of formal interviews. Instead, use them to listen and conduct research while simultaneously making a positive impression with a new member of your professional network. Your objective is simple – by the time you both complete drinking your coffee, you will want to impress the person on the other side of the table enough that they are motivated to act on your behalf and make calls and connections for you, ultimately helping you complete your one-of-a-kind jigsaw puzzle. Keith Green, a veteran marketing executive added, "Don't be afraid to use this tactic in reverse, either. I've lost count of how many cups-of-coffee I have had over the years with people who were looking for a job and wanted to network. That said, many of those same people you made time for might be in a position to help you now in your career transition. So, seek those people out and ask them to meet for coffee."[16]

---

16. https://gritdaily.com/job-search/

LESSON 30

LEVERAGE LINKEDIN

"LinkedIn, when used correctly, can become a catalyst for career change," wrote Kate Jones. That statement is as true now as it's ever been. For many years, LinkedIn served mostly as a platform for connecting with other professionals. Someone would invite you to connect and you would respond and typically, that was the end of the conversation. Many then turned LinkedIn into a game to see how many connections they could amass. Now, LinkedIn has become such a powerful online platform that even Generation Z, those born starting in 1997, are recognizing its value as much as Instagram and Snapchat from a social perspective. There are approximately 500,000 recruiters on LinkedIn daily working to identify candidates to fill jobs. In a LinkedIn blog post from several years ago, titled, "Change Is In The Air: 7 LinkedIn Tips For Career Changers," Lindsay Pollack offered seven ways to leverage LinkedIn for those in a career transition:

1. Become an expert on the career you want to pursue

2. Optimize your LinkedIn profile for your new career

3. Join LinkedIn groups related to your career

4. Alert your network to your career change plans

5. Talk to anyone who works or has worked in the field you want to join

6. Sign up for LinkedIn job alerts

7. Make real world changes

The bottom line, LinkedIn is your owned media channel and you have the ability to be read and heard by as many influencers as you choose. You are the researcher, writer, editor and publisher. From mobilizing substantive connections to publishing thought leadership content, you must fully leverage LinkedIn. Jones concluded her post, writing, "Changing career direction can feel overwhelming, but it doesn't have to be. By taking the time to consider the relevant skills you've already honed, you will be able to smoothly pivot in a new direction. LinkedIn provides a ton of powerful tools to help you on your journey. With a well-targeted profile, you'll position yourself to make the change you desire.[17]

17. https://careerenlightenment.com/use-linkedin-support-career-change
https://blog.linkedin.com/2011/06/07/7-linkedin-tips-for-career-changers

LESSON 31

CASH IN YOUR FAVOR BANK

Throughout your career, you have not maintained an Excel spreadsheet detailing all the good deeds you have done for others, but you have helped many in your professional and social network, and now is the time to cash in on that favor bank. While the idea of the "favor bank" became part of our lexicon after it was introduced by Tom Wolfe in 1987 in *The Bonfire of the Vanities*, it is more relevant to you now more than ever in the midst of a career transition. Don Spetner writes, "The idea is that one should make 'deposits' into the favor bank, because inevitably it will be necessary to one day make a 'withdrawal.' It's an efficient and time-worn system. It's also one of the most effective engines for advancing a career." Borrowing from Spetner, the favor bank is also one of the most effective engines for successfully completing your career transition. So, now is the opportune time to take more than a moment to think of all the favors and acts of kindness you provided throughout your lifetime and your career to former colleagues, clients, classmates and vendors. Those individuals will be even more eager to support and assist you when you reach out to them to make a withdrawal. You can't take your favor bank with you when you leave this earth so start to spend some of that savings you accumulated because there is no better time than the present to cash in your favor bank. [18]

---

18. https://annenberg.usc.edu/research/center-public-relations/usc-annenberg-relevance-report/favor-bank

LESSON 32

MOBILIZE THE MASSES

It is critical to take time to brand yourself and get your resume and LinkedIn profile updated as well as identify your targeted companies. However, once these items are complete, it is essential that you leverage every channel that is available to you through networking. Here is a list of some resources you must leverage:

- Friends

- Family

- Former Coworkers

- Former College Classmates

- Neighbors

- Industry & Professional Associations/Groups

- Alumni Associations

- Vendor Contacts

- Former Consultants you engaged and/or worked with

- Government resources – unemployment, retraining/reskilling, etc.

- Fellow members of groups to which you belong

- Seek out and join and attend local job search and networking group meetings (check out meetup.com and other networking groups via sites like LandingExpert.com where a free comprehensive listing of networking groups can be found under Networking)

- Seek out and attend industry meetings, expo events and conventions

LESSON 33

RAPIDLY EXPAND YOUR NETWORK

There are a number of ways you can rapidly expand your network. First, identify a list of individuals to target to add as contacts to grow your network.

On LinkedIn, there are individuals who have self-identified themselves as LinkedIn Open Networker (referred to as LION's or simply Open Networker) as they are open to connecting with you. So, as you are looking at companies you are targeting, see if anyone there is a LION or Open Networker. Connect with former coworkers and fellow college alums. You can find these individuals quicker by using the LinkedIn search feature with filters set properly to help identify these individuals. LinkedIn supplies a functionality where you can upload your contacts from an email program like Outlook or Google Mail and it will automatically find their matching LinkedIn profile and send an invitation to them to connect with you on LinkedIn. When you are networking, always seek to be introduced and connected by your point-of-contact with two more individuals who you can follow-up with – these can be two recruiters, two individuals at companies you are targeting, two members who are involved in networking groups you are looking to join or attend and on and on. The trick is to make the most of each interaction and constantly be multiplying by two or more and growing your network along the way as you have these interactions.

LESSON 34

CONTENT IS KING: START BLOGGING & POSTING

" Content is King" may date back to a 1996 essay Bill Gates wrote for the Microsoft web site, but it is even more applicable in 2020 and beyond especially for those who are in a career transition. There is no rule that states content can only be created and distributed by leading companies, brands and marketing agencies. Every single individual has the ability, skill and power to produce engaging and compelling content that can not only be viewed, followed and shared, but also lead to that next career opportunity. Once you identified the industry or category where you want to demonstrate and share thought leadership, there are two easy ways to get started. First, via Twitter, make a daily commitment to research and share content that is relevant to the industry and organizations you are prospecting. Each morning after you wake-up, conduct a simple Google search and share all relevant industry news and provide commentary and analysis for select news. Don't start and stop your efforts in the morning. Continue tweeting throughout the day. Also, on Twitter, follow as many individuals as possible who are influencers in the industry and organizations where you want to work. Secondly, use your LinkedIn channel as a similar platform, but consider writing and posting longer form content including videos as well as sharing relevant industry news and stories. That same content you post on LinkedIn can then be amplified via your Twitter and even Facebook page. Finally, go one step further in your content production and distribution efforts and use a platform like Wix or any of the many do-it-yourself web site or blog sites and create your own web site and blog that focuses exclusively on the industry and organizations where you want to take your talents. Once you have your sites up and running, blog regularly. You are not writing *War and Peace.* You should be writing thought-provoking, pithy posts that are highly sharable. All of these actions take time, but ultimately, they will save you time making your job search more efficient. For a column for The Muse titled, "How My Personal Website Helped Me Land My Dream Job," Erin Greenawald wrote, "By getting yourself a URL and filling your site with keywords related to your field, you flip job searching on its head. No longer will you just be reaching out to recruiters—there's a better chance they'll find you through searches and reach out to you on their own." As Erin writes, by taking a content-centric approach, you just flipped your job search from reactive to proactive where potential employers will be reaching out to you. [19]

---

19. https://www.themuse.com/advice/how-my-personal-website-helped-me-land-my-dream-job

LESSON 35

SHAKE UP YOUR SOCIAL MEDIA

No longer think of Facebook, Instagram and Twitter as purely just social media sites to share fun photos from your family party or your date night with your significant other. Go beyond LinkedIn and use your social media channels to socialize your career transition. In an article for The Muse titled, "45 Things To Do On Social Media To Find Jobs," Erin Greenawald writes, "most people know how to use social media in their personal lives, but it actually has a lot of power to make (or break) your job search. Studies have shown that 92 percent of companies are using social media for hiring – and that three out of four hiring managers will check out a candidate's social profiles." Once word gets out that you are in between jobs, formally announce it on your social media channels. You never know who in your social media following may be the connector to your next opportunity. There are five times as many people on Facebook as there are on LinkedIn. Always keep your posts positive and even inspiring and motivating for your followers. As you participate in career networking group meetings or travel to new towns and locations for informal meetings and interviews, share your journey, quotes that may have inspired you and any learnings in a way that can positively impact your followers. Your social media channels are your owned media channels. You are the journalist, editor and publisher which means you have the power to socialize your career transition as you see fit... and believe me, the more engaging content you share, the more opportunities you will uncover.[20]

---

20. https://www.themuse.com/advice/45-things-to-do-on-social-media-to-find-jobs

LESSON 36

CONNECT WITH A CAREER SUPPORT GROUP

❝ To enhance their job search and make it more effective, many people are turning to the encouragement found in job clubs (or career support groups) for support, networking and sharing tips on job hunting, resume writing and interviewing. Many people find job clubs energizing and genuinely helpful in moving their job search forward." For example, if you were to live in central New Jersey, specifically in Monmouth County, you live less than a one-hour drive from no less than five career support groups who meet weekly or monthly on different days. In other words, there are many career support networking groups nationwide who are eager to have you attend their meetings, share your story and learn from their guest speakers and career and job prospecting experts. You will even learn from former members who have successfully secured a job and return to the meetings to share the secrets to their success. Even outside the in-person meetings, the groups are sharing information and insights via their web site, Facebook platform and LinkedIn channel. The Breakfast Club NJ, which started with two people having breakfast 18 years ago to discuss job searches has blossomed to more than 6,000 members, shares no fewer than 25-35 job openings each week with its members via their direct email system. Most importantly, career support groups offer an army of like-minded individuals to help you on your journey which will feel lonely at times. These groups provide camaraderie, assistance, inspiration and motivation when you need it most. Simultaneously, your professional network will expand significantly, and you will learn and transform personally and professionally with each meeting you attend. No one gets a reward for securing their next job on their own. Instead, join one or more career support groups and expedite your journey to your next opportunity while making new friends in the process. Please go to http://LandingExpert.com to see a lengthy list of job search and career networking groups.[21]

LESSON 37

SECURE SIDE GIGS

"Side gigs – no matter what form they take – are becoming a smart move both financially and career-wise." In today's society, side gigs are not a bad thing. They are actually becoming more popular with each passing year. There are probably more people in your personal and professional network who drive for Uber or Lyft as a side hustle than you even know. A side gig could be even more relevant to your career than driving for a ride sharing program. Just because you are looking for your next full-time opportunity doesn't mean you can't serve as a consultant in your industry or take on special projects at the exact same time. Consulting will keep your mind sharp and place you into an environment of collaboration with a larger team while adding more professional contacts that could be missing puzzle pieces to your search. There are many stories of individuals who were let go from their company and started consulting as a way to pay the bills until they realized the consulting projects were paying the bills better than their full-time job while offering greater work-life balance. Other side gigs could include adjunct teaching at your local college or writing for an industry trade web site. In other words, while your primary job is to secure your next job, don't do it in a vacuum with your blinders on. Instead, multi-task and secure side gigs to not only pay some bills, but to create more connections towards that next opportunity. If you do engage in a side gig while you are employed, ensure that it doesn't present a conflict of intertest to your primary employment.[22]

---

22. https://www.themuse.com/advice/4-questions-smart-people-ask-about-side-gigs-so-they-dont-lose-their-jobs

LESSON 38

BUILD A BRIDGE WITH A BRIDGE JOB

As you advance in your career, not every job needs to serve the same purpose as the previous job. Based on your life-stage, age, retirement savings and a number of other factors, bridge jobs could serve as a solution or they could bridge to entirely new opportunities. U.S. News & World Report writes, "people may be interested in looking for 'bridge jobs,' work opportunities that keep them busy (and making money) while allowing them to ease slowly into retirement." The article continues, "Bridge jobs are obviously helpful to older individuals who want to keep working. But they're also beneficial to employers, more of whom recognize the value of hiring and retaining experienced employees..." Use the transition in your career, whether planned or unplanned, to explore all opportunities – freelance (Upwork, Fiverr, etc.), consulting, starting your own business and even bridge jobs. It is opportunities like bridge jobs that keep you highly productive and highly collaborative while introducing you to more individuals who become part of your network and could serve as connectors to future opportunities.[23]

23. https://money.usnews.com/careers/applying-for-a-job/articles/2018-06-18/ how-to-find-a-bridge-job-or-second-career-before-retirement

LESSON 39

FREELANCING CAN BECOME FULL-TIME

❝ Whether you're doing minimal, part-time freelance projects for this client, or you're working close to a full-time schedule as their freelancer, there are several concrete steps you can take to turn a freelance client into a full-time employer," writes Brie Weiler Reynolds for a column titled, "How To Transition From Freelance Work To A Full-Time Position." Ultimately, you have your sights set on a full-time job with full-time pay and full-time benefits, but while you are searching for that opportunity, don't reject invitations to be a freelancer. "If there is one thing I would have done differently during my transition, I would have put myself 'out there' for freelance work. Once I made that approach an important part of my weekly career transition routine, it started to pay dividends. I formed my own LLC as a result and it potentially could lead to consulting being a full-time endeavor," said Keith Green, a marketing and public relations executive. Freelancing can put you right in the middle of an organization and you have the opportunity to immerse yourself in the business of a company while demonstrating that you can deliver value that drives business impact. Additionally, freelancing, like a bridge job, will introduce you to a significant number of new professional contacts who could serve as a connection point to your next full-time opportunity. [24]

---

24. https://lifehacker.com/how-to-transition-from-freelance-work-to-a-full-time-po-1700762612

LESSON 40

REVISE YOUR RESUME

We always like to say that when you ask 10 people for resume advice, you will receive 20 conflicting responses and conflicting direction. "The more people look at your resume, the better," commented Keith Green, a public relations and marketing executive. "I had countless people look at mine before a recruiter contact pointed out an error. It wasn't egregious, but it bothered me nonetheless. Part of the lesson is that some people are better at editing and some will simply take the time and care needed to review your credentials." Everyone has a take on the do's and don'ts of resume writing, but what should be included and the level of detail should be consistent with what is needed to successfully convey that you are a great candidate for the position being recruited for. A very important factor to your success is that the better you network, the lower the importance of your resume in the job search process. The reason for this, if you can arrange a recommendation from a resource that the hiring manager trusts directly, this is a critical factor towards increasing your probability of success in landing that opportunity. The reason this is critical is that as per Steven Covey, you are operating at the "Speed of Trust." Basically, you are tapping into the strength of the relationship that the individual who provided the recommendation has with the hiring manager. We have all heard that a recruiter or hiring manager literally spend seconds looking at resumes and determining who to submit as potential candidates. This also changes when a personal recommendation is involved. When revising the resume look to the future, not to the past, unless it is relevant to the opportunity you are seeking.

LESSON 41

GET CERTIFIED

C ertifications can help your candidacy. They demonstrate an assessment of one's level of competency in a given area or discipline by an independent authority. Just carefully look at the many certifications out there and limit your pursuit of certifications to those that would be most relevant to the job you are seeking. Perhaps go to a site like Indeed.com and pull some job requisitions that are consistent with the opportunity that you are seeking. Look across these job requisitions and see if any of them list certifications as required or suggested for the candidates that they are seeking. Now, it is getting easier to obtain certifications as many original equipment manufacturers (OEMs) that offer certifications in their products, services, and/or methodologies are now offering certification materials and tests for free via online training sites like Alison.com and among Massive Open Online Courses "MOOC." Several universities even offer the content of their courses for free to the public. Check with those who are established in your profession, your alumni office, former managers you reported to and solicit their thoughts if they feel certifications would be beneficial and if so, which ones in particular would be of help to you and your specific career goals.

LESSON 42

RECRUIT RECRUITERS

If only we had a penny from every job seeker we encountered who was frustrated with a recruiter, or that they didn't call them back, or give them the time they felt they deserved, we would be enjoying retirement on a beach somewhere. The truth is that time is money to recruiters and they have to use it wisely in order to hit metrics that measure their performance and drive the recruiter's compensation. There are several techniques that you can use that will help build your emotional bank accounts with those you are networking with while at the same time helping you establish a strong relationship with recruiters. Previously you were instructed to join professional job search and networking groups. These groups can help you with recruiters in a number of ways. First, ask those that you meet in the networking groups to suggest to you who they feel are the top recruiters and even ask if they would be willing to make an introduction to the recruiter on your behalf. Also, once you are speaking with the recruiter here is a technique that is a win/win for you, the recruiter, and those in your network. When speaking with the recruiter, ask them if they have a hard-to-fill position. Tell the recruiter you are a member of several networking groups and would be will-ing to distribute this hard-to-fill opportunity to your groups to help out the recruiter. The recruiter gets additional resource(s) to fill a tough-to-fill job opportunity and those you are networking with now have additional opportunities. Next time you call that recruiter to check on your candidacy they will be more willing to take your call and push for you as a candidate as you've gone above and beyond and helped them.

LESSON 43

ENLIST THE SUPPORT OF A CAREER COACH

As you are managing your opportunities, you need to do some analysis to determine what your strengths and weaknesses are so you can determine where you need to improve and if you may need some help doing so.

- Are you not getting interviews? You may benefit from engaging a career coach that specializes in improving your resume and/or branding. Also, you may want to attend networking group sessions specific to this aspect of job search.

- Are you not getting offers following interviews? You may benefit from engaging a career coach that specializes in improving your interviewing competency.

- Are recruiters not calling you back? You need to rethink how you are leveraging and interfacing with recruiters in your job search.

- Are you effectively using references? You need to work well with your references:

  " Gain their agreement to serve as a reference on your behalf

  " Review any opportunity that you will provide them as a reference in advance recapping the opportunity, who it is with, and why you would make a great candidate

" Keep them informed through each stage of the process so they understand and can be prepared and anticipating the contact reaching out

" Remember to thank them for their support regardless of the outcome and offer to reciprocate on their behalf if ever needed

If you consider engaging a career coach:

- Be clear on fees and what the service will consist of in tangible terms

- Request some references and/or ask for coach recommendations from your network

- Ask the coach what they specialize in and why you should select and collaborate with them

PART 3

THINK AND ACT STRATEGICALLY TO ACHIEVE SUCCESS

LESSON 44

BE A SEVEN PERCENTER

❝ According to the University of Michigan University Career Center, referrals account for just 7% of all job applicants but 40% of all hires." Take a few moments to comprehend that powerful statistic. The majority of your competition who is applying for the same job that you are targeting are simply submitting their resume online and hoping that someone calls them for an interview. But always remember, "Hope is not a strategy." Instead, be a seven percenter. In other words, take all the lessons in this book in an effort to be referred for an opportunity you are strategically targeting. Simple math will tell you that you do not want to be a 93 percenter. Referrals not only provide you a much better statistical chance of securing the job, but it also helps you bypass the dreaded ATS robots and advances you directly to the phase of the candidate screenings and interviews where you can demonstrate your case for the job via old school (Lessons 48-50), human interaction (H.I.). As we have highlighted in this book, no matter how technologically advanced the employee recruiting process has become, companies, big and small, still rely on human interaction to vet and select the winning candidate which is one reason why referrals often help secure the position in the end. [25]

---

25. https://pnpstaffinggroup.com/8-ways-can-increase-chances-getting-hired/

LESSON 45

IT'S NOT WHO YOU KNOW, IT'S WHO THEY KNOW

I am sure we are all familiar with the expression, "It's not what you know, but who you know." This is very true, especially when you find yourself searching and prospecting for your next job. However, IBM Futurist, TEDx speaker and best-selling author of the "goldfish" series of books regarding delivering optimal service to customers and employees, Stan Phelps, takes it one step further. Stan likes to say to those seeking their career opportunity, "It's not who you know. It's who they know." Stan's insightful expression captures the essence of LinkedIn. To truly leverage the power of LinkedIn is not simply to connect with your connections, but it's to have your connections ultimately connect you to their connections who are already working at companies that you are targeting and prospecting or at least external vendors and agencies who conduct business with those organizations. Like any winning chess player, strategically think several moves ahead with the goal of checkmating your opponent. In your case, checkmating means utilizing your pieces, your immediate personal and professional contacts, to logically connect you to as many as five or six other connections that will lead you to a hiring manager or the recruiter in the human resources department of the employer you are looking to be employed by. Ultimately, you want these new connections to think of you when a new opportunity arises. Set your vision well beyond your immediate contacts and you will set yourself up for success.

LESSON 46

CREATE YOUR OWN WORD CLOUD

As businesses and organizations do each and every day to visualize customer sentiment or the attitudes of their employees, design your own career transition word cloud, sometimes called a text cloud or tag cloud, to help you visualize any number of topics relevant to your job search. One of your word clouds could be a visual representation of your strengths and areas for improvement. Another word cloud could be a mapping of your top-20 target companies and organizations with the largest fonts representing your top-five or 10 prospects where you have the greatest number of connections. A third word cloud could consist of a side-by-side comparison of the skills and experiences that you highlight in your resume and LinkedIn profile compared to the requisites that are featured in the job opening description. Lisa Lepki writes, "Word clouds are fun to use as a visual aid... to underscore the keywords on which you're focusing." Consider a word cloud another tool in your arsenal to leverage that can help you visualize the communication and messaging that you are using in writing and verbally to successfully secure the next opportunity in your career. [26]

26. https://prowritingaid.com/art/425/What-the-Heck-is-a-Word-Cloud-and-Why-Would-I-Use-One.aspx

LESSON 47

UNDERSTAND WHAT YOU'VE DONE, NOT WHERE YOU DID IT

Too often, too many job seeking candidates prioritize the industry or category they worked in, and not the actual work they did, the successes they achieved, the business-building solutions they implemented and the skills they applied. Most, if not all of those experiences are highly transferable to other industries. In fact, many companies today recognize value in hiring individuals who can bring a fresh perspective from their past experience in a different industry. Place less of a focus on where you did your work and more of a focus on the work it-self, your case studies, the measurable impact you and your team had on the business. While it may be obvious that an accountant in one industry can transfer those skills and be an accountant in another industry, other occupations may not appear so obvious. There was an individual who worked for a nationally recognized transportation and travel company where he arranged special charters, trips and other unique travel for major corporations and professional sports teams. As he journeyed through his transition, he was focused exclusively on working for a travel company. He limited potential opportunities by limiting his perspective on his experience and skills. Once the light bulb went off and he real-ized what he really did was logistics and coordination for large numbers of people, he came to the realization that he could apply that to a wide number of industries and organizations - confer-ence and convention centers, stadiums and arenas, professional sports teams and major corporations. As you explore beyond the obvious on your journey, don't just look at where you worked, but delve deeper into what you actually did.

LESSON 48

H.I. BEATS OUT A.I.

While each day, there is more talk about Artificial Intelligence (A.I.), it is Human Interaction (H.I.) which will ultimately lead you to success in your career transition journey. One of the authors of this book, Mark Beal, expands upon that concept in a guest column he wrote for Dice.com. "No matter how innovative the hiring process has become with the infusion of Artificial Intelligence and Applicant Tracking Systems (ATS), Human Interaction (HI) will ultimately determine the candidates that get hired. In the past, the candidate screening process consisted of a series of face-to-face interviews before the winning applicant was hired. Now, thanks to advancements in technology, most employers are using ATS robots to rank applicants based on specific terms they use in their resume or are employing interactive platforms such as LaunchPad (which combines video interviewing, mobile technology and intelligent automation). If a job candidate successfully passes that tech-vetting gauntlet, they may have earned the chance to be interviewed by a computer or a chatbot before they ever have any actual human contact. However, I believe going 'old school' and prioritizing human interaction in the job prospecting process will lead to greater success for job applicants. The odds of an individual getting a job via an online job site application which typically utilizes ATS is just 1 out of 250, according to a University of Michigan study. However, an individual can take more of a human interaction approach to job-seeking: employee referrals only make up seven percent of applications, but 40 percent of hires. In other words, if an applicant leverages their network, they will drastically improve their chances of securing a job than if they solely rely on today's tech innovations which are screening candidates and oftentimes eliminating the best person for the job." PJ Brovak, a marketing communications veteran confirmed this in saying, "In my search for my next professional role, every one of my interview opportunities happened directly because of the relationships I built during my 20-year career."[27]

27. https://insights.dice.com/2019/04/26/human-interaction-beats-ai-first-job/

LESSON 49

BYPASS THE ROBOTS

As highlighted in Lesson 48, the job application process has gone hi-tech with the proliferation of Applicant Tracking Systems (ATS). While you will formally need to apply to just about every job by submitting your resume via an online application portal that uses ATS robots, you need to counter that by making a human connection with someone at the company. "Often you may not know someone within a target organization to whom you can send your resume, but more times than not you can find a second connection there as long as you're willing to invest the time to look. A friend of a friend, a former colleague's client, a cousin's cousin... there's almost always a way to get your resume into someone's hands, outside of the online submission, and you'll increase your chances of getting an interview substantially if you're willing to look," commented Jim Sias, a marketer who recently made a transition in his career. Applying to jobs today requires a one-two punch combination, but most applicants only rely on the initial jab by submitting their resume online, and never follow-up with the counterpunch. It is the counterpunch of following-up your formal submission by reaching out to your network to learn who can make a call on your behalf to a decision maker on the inside that will enable you to bypass the robots. Time-after-time, the majority of individuals who get invited to be interviewed and ultimately, win the job, know how to throw a powerful counter punch. Longtime human resources executive Liz Ryan provided a great glimpse behind the ATS curtain in a column she penned for *Forbes* titled, "How To Sneak Past The Online Application And Get The Job." Consider what she wrote as you submit your next application. "The people who staff the broken recruiting system, naturally, can't tell you 'Just go around the back way and forget the online application.' They're not allowed to say that. They have to say 'No, you must follow the rules,' but they know it's not true. Hiring managers have problems. They are desperate for talent. They don't want to receive a stack of resumes to review six to eight weeks after they run a job ad. They want to hire someone now! Why shouldn't they hire you?" As you get frustrated with ATS technology, remind yourself of the approach Ryan recommends.[28]

---

28. https://www.forbes.com/sites/lizryan/2015/08/03/how-to-sneak-past-the-online-application-and-get-the-job/#172c84d42299

LESSON 50

ACHIEVE ATS SUCCESS

Applicant Tracking Systems (ATS) have numerous nuances that one must be aware of prior to submitting applications for jobs as there are many rules that if you are not aware, can keep your submittal from ever being seen by the potential employer so you will never even be considered. Large employers are more apt to use an ATS as it automates their ability to publicize their open positions and is an easy way to obtain a lot of candidates and they won't have to compensate a recruiter or other third party while also helping the employer be EEOC compliant.

The following is a list of a few of the top ATS solutions:

Taleo	Workday
Brassring	iCIMS
SmartRecruiters	JazzHR

If you're applying to a large firm, the probability is that you are doing so through an ATS. Also, if you are applying through an online form, you're more than likely doing so through an ATS. Even LinkedIn and Indeed use an ATS. Recruiters use ATS to filter resumes by searching for key skills and titles. The recruiters will craft a search so it can contain multiple terms. For example, they might perform a complex search that contains a combination of titles and skills to identify candidates for the job. You can reverse engineer keywords for your resume by doing a marketing analysis of identifying a dozen job requirements consistent with the opportunity you are seeking and identifying and reusing the words that the recruiters use in their job requirements. Resume formatting is critical to your success with an ATS. Keep section headings simple, use consistent formatting for your work history and dates, avoid tables, and use a .docx or .pdf file format. Understanding the requirements of an ATS and adhering to them when creating your "qualified submissions" is a great way to improve the success of your job search efforts.

LESSON 51

MAKE QUALIFIED SUBMISSIONS

What is a qualified submission? A qualified submission includes the following steps:

Step 1 – Research and target a company.

Step 2 - Once a position is found that you are a strong candidate for and have strong interest in, you need to work your network aggressively to find someone at the target company to provide insight on the firm so you understand the culture, how levels work, related pay by level, and quite possibly get you a introduction directly into the hiring manager.

Step 3 – Make your case for your candidacy for the opportunity with your resume by factually reordering bullets, expanding or collapsing points as to their applicability to requirements of position so that clearly your experience, education and skills highlight that you meet the requirements as applicable

Step 4 – Create a T Letter (see Lesson 65) as part of your cover letter.

Completing these four steps so that you have a "qualified submission" takes time and it is hard work, but the job search is about quality, not quantity. If you take the time to perform the steps required of a qualified submission and strive to make at least one qualified submission a day you will be happy to see the positive results that you will have in the form of a number of interviews by following the formula and creating "qualified submissions." This will increase your probability of landing as quickly as you can and keeping you focused on those positions that you are qualified for at companies you are targeting because you are a cultural match.

LESSON 52

MANAGE YOUR OPPORTUNITIES EFFECTIVELY

If you approach your job search correctly, you should be juggling many opportunities at one time. The challenge is to transform from simply juggling to effectively managing those opportunities. You can use a shareware product or something as simple as Microsoft Excel that many of us already use for other projects. The approach for effectively managing your opportunities is simple:

Create a spreadsheet or database and make each column or field applicable to common information you need to manage each opportunity. Here are some suggestions for columns/fields to get you going:

Name of Employer

Title of Position

Date you found the job posted

Contact at Firm

Contact at Firm's Information (email, phone, etc.)

Version of Resume and Cover letter submitted

Networking contact for this Target Firm

Networking Contact's Information

Date for follow-up communication

Date you initiated your candidacy

Status: In progress, interview, interview completed, informed no longer being considered

Notes: Free form field of documenting each interaction with the employer, recruiter and other gatekeepers

LESSON 53

MASTER TARGETING TECHNIQUES

So, you are about to embark on your job search journey. What's the first thing we do when we want to go on a trip? When we get into the car, the first thing we do is we enter the coordinates for our destination in the GPS. In your job search, the coordinates for your destination are the companies that you are targeting. These are companies that you have spent quality time analyzing to determine that you have an interest in pursuing them as an employer. During a job search, the companies you target may change as you will become apprised of new employers that you may decide to add to your list of targeted companies and some firms may have to be removed from additional information learned (perhaps a recent bad earnings report and/or poor financial outlook for the firm, announcement of workforce reduction at the firm, etc.). Having a list of target companies will focus your job search efforts to those firms you are targeting so that your daily efforts are guided. It is also essential when networking as this will help members of your network assist you more effectively.

LESSON 54

IDENTIFY YOUR TOP 20 TARGETS

Career coach Chrissy Scivicque writes in her blog, "All too often, job seekers take a 'spray and pray' approach to the search. They simply 'spray' their resume out in as many different directions as possible, and then 'pray' to get a call. Sadly, this strategy often leads to a lot of frustration and wasted time. A targeted job search tends to be the more fruitful approach. This means that you go into it knowing exactly what kind of role you're looking for and you have a list of organizations you're interested in." Based on your desired industry and category, as well as the region where you want to live, commute and work or are willing to move to for work, strategically identify and rank as many as 20 or 25 companies and organizations that you would like to make your next home. Of course, this requires more research - research in your region, research about corporate structure and culture and research about employee turnover rates, the vision of the leadership team and any information that indicates that the organization is continuously transforming and keeping pace or ahead of the marketplace and the competition. There will be other reactive opportunities that will come your way, but these 20-25 companies are now your prospects who you are going to strategically and proactively target like you are the world's leading sales representative. Without taking the strategic initiative to research and identify your specific prospects, you are significantly limiting your career transition campaign. You would only be employing a reactive approach which means your simply standing by waiting for the phone to ring. Now, you have a two-tiered proactive and reactive sales prospecting approach that will significantly expedite the journey to the next destination in your career.[29]

29. https://www.ivyexec.com/career-advice/2017/targeted-job-search-identify-target-companies/

LESSON 55

GO WHERE IT'S WARM

Valerie Schlitt writes, "Warm leads have, at the very least, raised their hand and expressed interest in your offering. While warm leads vary in degrees of temperature, from lukewarm to borderline hot, they all have two things in common. One, they hold great potential for future sales. Two, they require nurturing and cultivation to keep them from turning cold again. Ideally, those warm leads will one day turn hot." If you have ever held a job in sales or had to lead the new business for your agency or organization, you always start with your warmest leads and prospects. In other words, as you identify and rank the companies that you want to prospect and target, prioritize those where you have the most connections inside the organization and outside in the form of external vendors and agencies. Consider other factors as well including your experience and skills versus the business model of the organization. For example, if you have had a career in consumer marketing and there is a company that is looking for a marketing veteran with a focus on business-to-business, that may not be the warmest lead even though it is a marketing role. Once you have identified your top-20 or 25 companies to target and prospect, rank them based on a warm-to-cold spectrum. Review each company and consider a number of factors like those we mention in this lesson and rank the warmest prospects in your top-five. Those top-five prospects should be the ones that you invest the majority of your time and resources as those are your warmest leads. [30]

---

30. https://www.business.com/articles/prevent-warm-leads-turning-cold/

LESSON 56

PURSUE YOUR PROSPECTS

Once you have identified the right 20-25 companies for you, it's time to prospect them proactively and strategically. Aside from simply learning what openings they are attempting to fill, you need to think bigger. You need to share these prospects with your closest allies in your network. You need to uncover which of your allies know anyone either working at the company or one-step removed, a preferred vendor or an external agency. "During my transition, I created a roadmap that identified the industries, locations and brands that not only aligned with my experience, but made sense for me personally - quality of life, commute, potentially finishing my career here. And for those brands that I didn't have an 'in' with, I resourcefully leveraged my network to help make those introductions," remarked PJ Brovak, a marketing communications veteran. Ultimately, your goal is to gain access to their offices or headquarters. In other words, you want to be able to walk right through the front door knowing your name is already on the security list. The only way to accomplish that significant step is to have one of your allies introduce you to someone on the inside with the simple objective of securing that informal cup-of-coffee meeting. In securing that informal meeting, you not only gain access to the company, but you get the opportunity to walk the halls and observe the culture first-hand. Are all the employees quietly hiding in their cubicles or are you witnessing collaboration, brainstorming, high-energy and even fun? Yes, you are allowed to have fun and smile and laugh at work. Most importantly, you are attempting to learn as much as you are able about the hiring and decision-making process. Additionally, you are attempting to make such a positive impression that the individual you meet with feels compelled to walk you and your resume right down the hall to the recruiters in the human resources department. Even if that doesn't happen, you want to establish an ally on the inside who will now keep you top-of-mind when future opportunities arise.

LESSON 57

TRANSFORM YOUR RESUME

If you are like the majority of people, you have not even looked at your resume since the last time you secured your last job. So, don't simply just blow the dust off it and add three new sub bullets for your latest experience. Instead, conduct some more research regarding resumes that are compelling and ultimately make the final cut. Most importantly, reach into your network and identify one or more contacts in human resources and recruiting. Individuals in these roles review hundreds of resumes weekly. They can quickly and effectively tell you how to transform your resume from a style and content perspective. Once you have applied their resume recommendations, email your resume to several decision makers in your network across a variety of industries. Since they may work in categories outside your expertise, you are looking for a gut reaction rather than the technical commentary you will receive from a recruiter. Always remember that your resume is a living and breathing document. It is never completed. For every job you apply to, you may tweak your resume to reflect and highlight relevant experience that is applicable to that specific job opening.

In an article titled, "56 Resume Tips To Transform Your Job Search," Jon Shields emphasizes the importance of developing and maintaining a central resume that houses all your critical experience and information. "Consider maintaining a master resume or career management document. Think of this as a giant, overstuffed curriculum vitae. It should contain all your job duties, all your accomplishments, all the tools that you used– everything you can think of for every job you've ever had. Maintaining a document like this can provide a great starting point for new resumes, ensuring that you don't forget anything important while allowing you to simply delete content rather than rewriting."[31]

---

31. https://www.jobscan.co/blog/resume-tips/

LESSON 58

UNDERSTAND DATA AND DETAIL FOR LINKEDIN AND RESUME

Your LinkedIn profile and your resume are two very sepa-rate artifacts critical to your job search and should be complementary but not contain information at the same level of detail. Please take notice that most employers will now do a digital search of your information and if the digital data disputes what is on your resume it could result in the employer eliminating you from consideration for the position. Also, LinkedIn has more than 500,000 recruiters who are searching for candidates for jobs that they are seeking to fill so it is critical you understand how they use the product and present your information in such a way so you are easily found by the recruiters and seen as a match for the positions that they are recruiting for.

How should your LinkedIn profile and resume be similar?

Your LinkedIn profile should be complementary to your resume in that it should reconcile to your resume at a higher level of detail. You should have the same jobs, job titles, in the same timeframe between the two artifacts, however, the level of detail supporting your explanation of the responsibilities at the position should be high level on LinkedIn but more detailed and in PAR format (see Lesson 66) on your resume.

How should your LinkedIn profile and resume be dissimilar?

On LinkedIn, there is a prescribed format for the profile and there are additional attributes to your profile (skills, endorsements, recommendations, awards) that exist that aren't present on your resume that you want to exploit to your advantage in your LinkedIn profile. Carefully choose those data items that will help recruiters identify you as a potential match for the position they are seeking to fill.

LESSON 59

DEVELOP YOUR JOB SEARCH TOOL

" Smart job seekers know to go beyond the obvious tools to find the perfect position." One of those ways of going beyond is to create a simple one-page job search tool that is not a resume. Your resume or your CV is the formal biography for your career that highlights your education, experience and special skills. It is what potential employers formally require when you apply for a job. However, a resume or a CV is not going to be helpful to individuals in your professional network who you are seeking assistance. For that, you need to create a job search tool. Think of your resume as a document that speaks to your past, while a job search tool offers a vision for your future. It will also be the best one-page document to inspire and mobilize your allies to assist you. Your job search tool consists of a few key sections. First, it should include all your contact information as well as LinkedIn address and even your Twitter handle and links to your personal web site and blog hosting site if you have either. It should also provide four glimpses into your future - the region or markets where you would like work, the categories or industries you are targeting, the companies you are prospecting and finally, the types of job titles you are pursuing or are interested in pursuing based on your level of experience. Once you develop and distribute this highly effective job search tool, your allies in your network now know exactly how and where they can help you. A resume does not do that. Ultimately, you want everyone who you share your job search tool with to identify at least one contact working at one

of the companies on your target list or at least someone closely affiliated with one of those companies, and you want them to make a formal introduction to that individual. In the end, your resume may help you get your next job, but your job search tool is going to be the key that opens the door to companies you were previously locked out of. "One of my much admired mentors told me this one pager was critical to my search for two reasons: 1) it will help you focus on what it is that you truly want with your next professional role and 2) it will help your network effectively and efficiently advocate on your behalf when recommending you to their network," commented PJ Brovak, a marketing communications veteran.[32]

---

32. https://www.cheatsheet.com/money-career/underrated-job-search-tools-find-perfect-career.html/

LESSON 60

GO BACK TO SCHOOL

All of a sudden, you have some time on your hands. Don't waste it. Instead, go ahead and do some of those things you pushed off, but never had the time. In today's online world of education, going back to school can take on many forms. It can be as simple as logging on to a one-time only webinar taught by an author, actor or athlete. It could mean getting that certificate in search engine optimization or some other subject matter that will bolster your resume and improve your chances of securing your next opportunity. It could mean attending a guest lecture being given by a power player in your industry and meeting that individual may bridge the gap to a company you are targeting. Or, it could mean earning a mini MBA or a master's degree while you simultaneously seek your next opportunity. It could even mean going back to school to serve as an adjunct professor at a local community college or university where you can leverage your career experiences while potentially launching a new career in education which many people have accomplished as part of their own career transition. Nicole Fallon writes, "It's never too late to change career paths. If you're not happy, you deserve the chance to take a different road – no matter what that entails. For some career changers, this means returning to school." Whatever the reason, be a student for life and let new learnings and lessons take you places you never imagined. Continuous learning has never been as important as it is now given the unprecedented pace of change and volume of change that we are experiencing.[33]

---

33. https://www.businessnewsdaily.com/7064-back-to-school-career-change.html

LESSON 61

THINK BIG AND START A SMALL BUSINESS

‟People are not born entrepreneurs. They normally become one after a problem is presented to them. Some are trying to solve a common issue we face, while some are trying to change the world. Throughout my entrepreneurial journey, one of the most common catalysts I have found for entrepreneurship has been associated with job loss.” Mike Wood wrote this for *Entrepreneur* after losing his job and starting his own marketing agency. Depending on a number of critical factors include your lifestage, the amount of money you have invested, your age in relation to the number of years you want to work, your passions outside your day job and many others, you don't necessarily have to transition from one job to another job. You can transition from a job to your own business. One example is a longtime public relations veteran in the real estate industry who was impacted by a corporate downsizing and consolidation. While his first reaction was to find his next job, as he immersed himself in his transition, he realized that he could leverage his many years as a public relations and communications specialist in real estate and launch his own public relations agency. Several years later, his agency is thriving and he is enjoying greater work-life balance than he did when he worked full-time for a large corporation. If you are in a position to do so, seriously consider leveraging your past experiences as well as your passions and hobbies and start your own small business or consultancy. Use this opportunity to set your own rules and write your own business plan and determine your company's own visions and mission.[34]

34. https://www.entrepreneur.com/article/280636

LESSON 62

EXERCISE YOUR ENTREPRENEURIAL SPIRIT

For many years, you have relied on a larger power to pay your salary and benefits. You have leaned on big business or perhaps a small business to survive. Can you imagine a world where you generate your own revenue and you don't rely on an employer to help you pay your bills? You and you alone can control your own destiny by exercising your entrepreneurial spirit. There are millions of individuals who have left corporate America and who have started their own business and ignored the doubters who told them it would be impossible. A business does not have to be a traditional brick and mortar store. In today's digital world, a business can be launched and sustained in the smallest room in your house using a mobile phone, personal computer and your entrepreneurial mindset. Before you race to your next job, evaluate all your options and seriously consider mobilizing all the experience, expertise and intellectual capital you have accumulated to support your own company or consultancy. David Siroty, a senior public relations and marketing executive shared his inspirational story. "When I was downsized from my job – something that corporate America seems to love doing to all of us – a friend who owned his own business doubted my ability to start my own consultancy. He didn't think I had the entrepreneurial spirit or the guts to do it. I did it. I am now in my third year of leading my own company. No one is secure anymore, but now I control my own destiny and I realize that there is plenty of fun and interesting work out there for me to handle and make a nice income in the process."

LESSON 63

CONTINUE TO SERVE OTHERS

❝ I heard a famous music industry executive say in an interview that if you are in the service business, you always need to be of service," remarked PJ Brovak, a marketing communications veteran. "That rang true to me not only in my profession, but during my search. You would be amazed how the people responded to my willingness to put them first." While your journey to your next job opportunity should be your primary focus throughout your transition, part of that focus can include assisting others in your professional and personal network who will call on you because of your skills, experiences and relationships. It may seem odd that they are asking for your service knowing you are out-of-work and seeking your next job, but serving them is all part of a proactive mindset and approach as you never know what your service may lead to or who you may meet in the process. Mahatma Gandhi said it best, "The best way to find yourself is to lose yourself in the service of others." A major element of your career transition journey is "finding yourself" and learning and discovering more about who you want to be in the next chapter of your career. That discovery will come in many forms, but it will also come in serving and helping others while you simultaneously seek assistance and support from your network. Serving others will also contribute not only to your "favor bank" which we feature in Lesson 31, but more importantly, it will contribute to helping you maintain a positive attitude, perspective and mindset.

LESSON 64

REMIND YOURSELF WHAT YOUR PASSIONS WERE WHEN YOU STARTED YOUR CAREER

As you journey through your career transition, take some quality time to remind yourself what your passions were when you launched your career. In other words, remind yourself what type of work you loved then and what passions have surfaced in the past few years. No one every dictated or legislated that you had to settle for a job that you disliked. If you take time to remind yourself of past and present passions, you might want to pursue that as one of the paths in your current job search. Your search does not have to be exclusively linked to your most recent job or solely to a certain industry. In a column titled, "6 Fresh Ways To Find Your Passion," Corrina Gordon-Barnes writes, "The path of passion is where you do things that scare you enough, without leaving you in a constant state of fear. Expand your comfort zone, rather than leaving it." So, get out of your comfort zone and scare yourself a bit. There is no better time than the present to immerse yourself in your passions, experiment and explore a variety of opportunities that could result in you starting to write the next chapter in your career.[35]

---

35. https://www.themuse.com/advice/6-fresh-ways-to-find-your-passion

LESSON 65

TAKE ADVANTAGE OF A T LETTER

C reating and leveraging a T Letter in your job search is a critical artifact that will greatly enhance your probability of success in not only obtaining interviews but can also be the difference in your being selected over the other candidates to fill the position.

The best part of a T Letter is how easy it is to create one:

Step 1 – Split the paper down the middle lengthwise

Step 2 – Take a printed copy of the job requirements and highlight all the items the employer is seeking and list them down the left side of the page

Step 3 – On the right side of the page, next to each job requirement, list your experience, skills and/or education you have that demonstrate that you meet the requirement

This T Letter document is gold as it basically makes the case that you are qualified for the job that you have initiated your candidacy for. Add a paragraph on top and at the bottom and you now have a great cover letter. Whether this goes to a gatekeeper in HR or the hiring manager themselves, they can now clearly and effectively see that you are a candidate that meets the job requirements they seek and your probability for being selected to come in and interview for the position has increased substantially. Another great thing to do is bring a copy of your T Letter to your interview as a leave behind for the hiring manager. Think of it this way - everyone who was invited to interview should meet the requirements for the position. However, you just provided the hiring manager with a well-thought through list of why you are an exact match for the position. If the hiring manager simply "reuses" this as their justification to their boss as to why you were selected, you just provided your candidacy another edge over the other finalists.

LESSON 66

PRACTICE PARS

C reating and effectively leveraging Problem/Action/Result (PARs) are critical to multiple steps throughout your job search process. Let's explore why and how they are important to your candidacy. The master version of your resume should contain many PARs that cover all the experience related to your responsibilities of the various positions that you have held. You can then pick and choose from this master list of PARs when you are applying to a position by selecting those that are applicable to the position that you are applying to. Considering the specific position that you are applying, you may want to reword or clarify certain aspects so that information that pertains to the opportunity is very clear and easily understood. The PAR, if used correctly, should also serve as the basis for your answers during the interview. This allows you to explain how you encountered similar challenges in your career previously, how you were able to meet and overcome these challenges, and the benefit and results you were able to realize for your employer and their clients. Please remember that when you are sharing this information with the interviewer be very aware of any verbal signs or body language they are providing. Also, be clear to delineate if the accomplishment was yours personally or if you worked as part of a team or led the team to achieve them. If they seem to be losing interest, wrap-up the answer or ask the interviewer if you can further explain a specific aspect of the question that they posed. Always have some well thought through questions for the interviewer in advance so you can use these to find out more about the position and the employer that may not have been covered in the job description and any other information that you were provided.

LESSON 67

DEVELOP A POINT SYSTEM TO MEASURE YOUR PROSPECTING

As you go through your job search transition, you need a way in which to gauge your level of effort and success. Many will look at whether they have obtained a job offer as the key to whether their job search is successful or not. Achieving a job offer is the ultimate objective of your effort, but if you have that as your only measure of success it will lead to a long process and contribute to the many ups and downs you will face. So, what we suggest instead is to look at all the activities that you must perform during a job search which includes, but are not limited to:

- Adding new contacts to your network

- Identifying and attending networking meetings

- Identifying and establishing relationships with recruiters

- Creating and honing your resume

- Developing PARS (Problem, Action, Results) statements for your resume and interviewing

- Honing your interviewing skills and preparing for interviews

- Researching and identifying strong potential employers to target

- Identifying and networking with individuals who work currently at, previously worked at, or can introduce you to individual(s) that work at your targeted employers
- Making qualified submissions (making a case with your resume and T-Letter) for jobs you are strong match
- Turning unknown to known opportunities
- Going on interviews
- Following up after interviews with thank you letters

Now, assign a point value to each of these activities and then dig down and set an objective that if you work really hard and smart, how many points you can realistically expect to achieve on a weekly base. Track your progress and how many points you accumulate each week and if you hit your target, celebrate and reward yourself in some way. Maybe you would like to see a movie, maybe you enjoy reading a good book, but do something for yourself that recognizes the hard work and that you accomplished your goals for that week. Also, if you have a significant other, share with them your goals, activities, and accomplishments so they can understand all the work you are putting in. Communication with a significant other and family during a job search is essential as in the end, you are all affected by the outcome.

LESSON 68

TURN THE UNKNOWN INTO KNOWN OPPORTUNITIES

How does one go about seeing a job posted and then turn this opportunity that you have found from an unknown to a known opportunity? Thankfully social media exists and is critical in helping us with this task as we now have a great resource like LinkedIn which allow us to operationalize and leverage the six degrees of separation. So, to begin with, we need to know the name of the firm that the job opportunity is for. Then, using LinkedIn as an example, here is a scenario you can follow to achieve it.

1. Go to LinkedIn and see who you are connected to at the firm who posted the job:

    a. If you have a 1st level connection at the firm, you should go through and make your case for your candidacy by doing a qualified submission.

        i. Produce a T-Letter as part of your cover letter

        ii. Make the case with your resume for your candidacy for the position

    b. Reach out to your connection and request time to speak with them and explain you are seeking to learn more about the firm/employer.

    c. During the discussion ask questions about the culture, what levels exist and how they work as well as related pay structures. You may be lucky enough that your contact can even explain the group in which the job is within and the hiring manager. Then share the specific opportunity you are interested in and share the case as to why you feel you would be a strong match.

2. If you don't have a level 1 connection at the targeted firm, you can:

   a. See if you have a level 2 connection that can in-turn request that they make an introduction for you to someone at the firm.

   b. Leverage your network on LinkedIn, Facebook, and other channels to network your way into the firm to simply have discussions and learn more about firms you are targeting and to establish contacts at these targeted firms. Send a brief email to the networking groups members that you are targeting XYZ firm as a potential employer and would appreciate if anyone who works there, previously worked there, or knows someone there can make an introduction for you.

LESSON 69

MANAGE MULTIPLE OPPORTUNITIES

A great problem for anyone in a job search is to have too many opportunities but you must be careful to maximize your reach but not beyond your ability to effectively manage the universe of opportunities you have and are actively working. As previously suggested in Lesson 52, carefully keep opportunity related details in a spreadsheet that you constantly update and mine the sheet so you understand when your interviews are, what follow-ups you committed to and when they are to be done. It is critical you effectively manage all these contacts, opportunities, and interactions during your job search as again you are leaving a lasting impression with each interaction. Missing returning a call on a specific day and the time that you committed to getting the date and time of an interview wrong will negate all the time and work you invest in identifying and securing those opportunities so you want to ensure you make the most of each opportunity and are fully prepared to do so. Also, share your progress and your tracking sheet with those you are close to - parents, spouse, significant other, children. You need to realize that they are going through your job search with you. It's critical to share and communicate what you are going through as they may be able to provide good advice or suggestions for improvement. They can share in your gains and help pull you through the tough times.

LESSON 70

FIT THE CULTURE

Once a potential employer has decided on you as a candidate and an interview has been set, the major factor in determining who gets selected to fill the opportunity from the slate of candidates is the one who is the best cultural fit. It is critical that you really pull out all your stops in networking to turn this unknown into a known opportunity. You need to identify someone who currently works or previously worked at the targeted firm so that they can explain to you more about the firm, its' values, history, unwritten rules, vision and culture. Ideally, you would have liked to have gone through all of this when you were going through your process of researching your targets to prospect, but the possibility exists a job opportunity may present itself that looks good but isn't with one of your targeted firms. Then, you must kick your primary research into high gear to accomplish your diligence on the firm quickly. The best way to do so is through your network. If you don't have someone who is a direct contact currently working at this potential future employer, try to use a mutual contact to gain an introduction to an individual on the inside who can schedule a conversation. Another alternative is to send a purposely short email to your network requesting if anyone currently works or had previously worked at the employer that you are targeting or knows of someone that is there and simply ask that they contact you directly. Once you have qualified this contact you can then work with them one-on-one.

LESSON 71

PLAY BY THE PROSPECTING RULES

There are many guidelines that you need to be aware of and follow which are not documented anywhere related to a specific job search that can have a critical impact on you getting the job you are pursuing.

Rule 1 – Once you apply to a position through a recruiter, you are now locked into association with that recruiter at the targeted firm for a certain period of time (usually six months). So, if you find another opportunity that interests you at that same firm, unless you go through the same recruiter it may disqualify your candidacy and doing so may extend the timeframe you are now locked into that recruiter at that firm.

Rule 2 – If you are using a recruiter at a targeted firm, run everything through them as they are your partner in the opportunity. If you go around them without their knowledge it could have negative consequences on your candidacy

Rule 3 – Always tell the truth and don't embellish or fabricate experience, skills or competencies as even if you land the position you won't be able to meet the requirements of your responsibilities.

Rule 4 – Never stop networking. Once you land, continue growing your network among both those in your new firm but also keep your personal network alive and growing as well. You never know when a transition could come again.

Rule 5 – Give to those you are networking with to the greatest extent possible as it will come back to you many times over.

Rule 6 – Your job search will be the hardest job you ever have so it's critical you remain focused, keep up your regular qualified submissions, and follow-through on known submissions whenever able, and work to set aggressive, but attainable objectives weekly.

Rule 7 – If you share your resume with a recruiter, be very specific that they aren't to share with a prospective employer without your knowledge and consent.

Rule 8 – Think out-of-the-box and be innovative and creative in prospecting your targets and ensure they have positions consistent with your passion.

Rule 9 – One of the hardest things is to deal with is the uncertainty, but don't let the uncertainty cause you to take actions that aren't consistent with the best practices we shared as they will have a good chance of extending your time in search.

LESSON 72

GAIN THE EDGE OVER OTHER CANDIDATES

Throughout these lessons, there are numerous items all meant to give your candidacy an edge throughout the job search process. Each individual item only gives you a slight edge, but when they are combined together, they give your candidacy a significant edge in aggregate. This is intended to recap those items that will give you an edge and when they all converge, give your candidacy a significant edge over the other candidates being considered:

Making the case with your resume – makes it easier to see you as a match for the opportunity and increases your chance of gaining an interview.

Turning an unknown to a known opportunity – getting a recommendation or introduction directly into the hiring manager is the holy grail for helping a job seekers candidacy. Achieving this will substantially increase the probability of success.

PARs – this is the basis for your conversations during the interview and provides tangible evidence you've been there and tackled the challenge and can deliver measurable value.

T Letter – methodically shows that you meet all the published requirements for the position and provides the hiring manager with the justification of why you were hired that they can in turn use with their manager to justify hiring you.

Effectively leveraging a recruiter in your search – know the do's and don'ts and find out which recruiters are used by your targeted company. Often, a potential employer has a limited approved list of recruiters that they will work with who are on their approved vendor list. Understanding this may be the critical piece of information to help you gain access to the recruiter that you are targeting.

Networking Impactfully – build and strengthen your network with every interaction. Never stop networking even after landing both at your new employer and outside of work. Remember the strength and reach of your network is the only rainy day insurance policy your career will ever have.

LESSON 73

INCREASE YOUR INTERVIEW SELECTION CHANCES

Y ou need to leverage these critical elements in unison to increase your probability of being selected from hundreds possibly thousands of other candidates just to be interviewed:

- Build a strong and extensive network that you can leverage through turning an unknown to known opportunity as well as increasing the amount of people who know of you and know of your value proposition which may lead to uncovering unknown jobs and help in identifying and tapping the hidden job market.

- Make the case for your candidacy with your resume providing all the information clearly so that the critical gatekeepers see you as a strong match for the open position.

- Carefully craft PARs on your resume that demonstrates your competency to meet the requirements of the position listed in the job description.

- Use a T Letter effectively as part of your strategic approach to writing and submitting a cover letter.

- Transform this unknown opportunity into a known opportunity.

- Get someone to deliver a reference and recommendation by phone, email or in-person to the hiring manager. Prepare any reference in advance by sharing the job description of the position you are pursuing. Also, share the resume and your cover letter including the T Letter. If you prepare your reference thoroughly, they will be able to speak much better when providing your recommendation. Additionally, keep those providing references apprised. Did you get the opportunity? Are there other opportunities you may need them to serve as a reference for?

- If a recruiter is involved, have them present you as the preferred candidate.

LESSON 74

RETHINK RELOCATION

If you are considering taking a position that requires relocation and/or relocation is your priority and finding a job in the city you are planning on relocating to, there are many variables that you need to consider and research to ensure you are making an informed decision and have all the needed information in order to do so effectively. Learn if you have a family member or someone in your network in the target location who can provide insight to the many questions you may have regarding the new geography that you are considering moving to. In addition to the direct questions such as home prices, property taxes, state taxes, and the commuting situation, think of all the indirect considerations such as the quality of doctors in the immediate area, proximity to hospital(s), and other considerations that may be important to you. Research and learn if there are job search and networking groups in the area you are targeting and start getting involved with them, even if you can only do so remotely, so you can get many perspectives on the area that you are considering. There are countless references at the library that you can leverage to help gather the information you need regarding the area that you are considering relocating to. It's critical you gain as much insight into relocation as possible so that you can make the best informed decision.

LESSON 75

PRIORITIZE THE NEED FOR THE SPEED OF TRUST

The reason connections are so important in job search is that the connection's level of strength of relationship with the contact you are targeting can be a significant asset to your search. If you think back to most of the jobs you have had, many, if not all, were secured through networking. Networking is essential to your job search in a number of ways. It is critical for turning an unknown into a known opportunity, for getting a recommendation to the hiring manager, but to us, most importantly it unlocks the unknown job market. Managers may not have a job requisition created for every position that they have budgeted and/or may have discretion into how they meet the demand. Thus, when you are networking, and someone trusted by a hiring manager introduces you they are now meeting you in a different light. It isn't to measure how you fit with a job requisition. It is listening to the value you bring and the needs that they have. That is the unknown job market. So, if the hiring manager establishes a connection with you and they have a need, don't be surprised if you find yourself in an informal interview without a job requisition. The great thing about this is that if the recruiter really wants to hire you, they may not even post the job and consider other candidates. These are two more reasons why having targeted companies and networking impactfully are so critical to the success of your job search.

LESSON 76

IDENTIFY THE HIDDEN JOB MARKET

You may have heard in life that, "it's not important what you know, but it's more important who you know." After many years of spearheading one of the nation's leading job search and networking groups, The Breakfast Club NJ, Frank Kovacs has heard this old saying evolve to "It's important who knows you." This is the crux of successfully unlocking the hidden job market. Throughout this book, we detail the critical importance of the following:

- Treating every interaction as an interview
- Always networking – "always be connecting"

It is critically important to consistently focus on expanding the number of people in your network – especially "who knows you" and your value proposition and brand. You can enlist the help of your entire network if you interact with them appropriately and build solid relationships so that they will be out there and ready to mobilize when opportunities arise consistent with your competency and they will recommend and/or consider you. Ultimately, you want to evolve your network to the point where the hiring manager "knows you" and is interested in you and the value that you can deliver. That is the brilliance that is in identifying the hidden job market.

LESSON 77

AVOID THE COMPENSATION CONVERSATION

We have all been there where we are just having the initial discussion regarding a position and either the recruiter or even the hiring manager may be asking us what are your salary requirements? Now you were having a great conversation and don't want to potentially derail this by discussing compensation too early and possibly kill your candidacy. The good news is that compensation has become so complex in today's environment that by answering this question as follows should provide you the latitude you need to avoid having it prematurely and delaying it to a time where it would be more appropriate.

We have had recruiters address the networking group and their suggestion has been to ask the potential employer's representative what the position was budgeted for and once they share, tell them if your salary requirements are within the range.

We prefer a slightly different tact where you explain to the employer representative that compensation has changed so significantly where salary is just one component and the proposed benefits and their costs are important in determining the salary needed. For example, is health coverage included or does the employee pay part and if so what percent and amount? This simple point can significantly sway total compensation as well as compensation elements such as if the company has a pension, if not 401K, and if so, what is the 401K match percent? Many times we have found the employer's representative sympathetic and they will then explain some of these details or the range for the job to see if it's in the ballpark.

Whichever tact you take, ensure that you provide the minimum information required as you don't want to negotiate until you have them convinced that you are the candidate they want. One final piece of advice, try to negotiate all the finer points with HR rather than with the hiring manager. Once you start working, you will need to work closely with the hiring manager, and you don't want anything to disrupt the relationship that you are forming.

LESSON 78

MANAGING MULTIPLE OFFERS

What a great problem to have – consider yourself blessed instead of looking at this as a quandary. At the beginning of your search, you want to make a list of attributes that you want to consider in the ideal position then rank and order them in priority and importance from most to least:

- Length of commute

- Salary of position

- Benefits that employer offers

- Where position is located

- Industry outlook for potential employer and its ranking in the industry

- Opportunity for advancement beyond current position

- Quality of work/life balance

- Nature of responsibilities

- Ability to work remotely

- Amount of vacation and PTO days

- Long term outlook of employer, industry

- Culture of organization

Then, once you have your multiple offers go back to this original list as it will remind you what you were seeking and what you considered important. Use this as the basis for comparing the different offers you received and to help in making a decision between them.

PART 4

MAKE MAJOR ADVANCES WITH MARKETING, RESEARCH AND PREPARATION

LESSON 79

SUPERSIZE YOUR
SKILLS ON LINKEDIN

The skills you carefully select to display on your LinkedIn profile and getting the endorsement of those skills and even how your order these on your LinkedIn profile are critical to the success of your candidacy. First, it is suggested that you pull approximately a dozen position descriptions for jobs you are interested in pursuing. The reason is to identify the top skills that the employers of these jobs are seeking. Then, if you possess these skills make sure that they are among those skills listed on your LinkedIn profile and work to get them endorsed. The best way to do so is to go to the profiles of current and/or former colleagues and others in your network and endorse their skills. Most times they will want to return the favor and will, in turn endorse your skills. You want to order your skills for different purposes at different times. Only the first three skills display in the default view of your LinkedIn profile. So, if you are a job seeker you want the top three you have seen on the job req's and/or those that support your brand the best. If you are in process of looking for endorsements, you may want to put those you are most seeking endorsement for on top as those seeking to endorse you will usually endorse those skills that are easiest to access. Finally, those skills that will label you as legacy even if well endorsed may be causing your brand more harm than good and if this is the case even if they are heavily endorsed it may be more in your interest to delete them then to keep them on your profile and potentially keeping you from securing the job you seek. This same logic applies to when you are doing a qualified submission. You want to include that information that "makes the case for your candidacy." If it isn't relevant to that point it becomes a detractor to the hiring manager and could work negatively for your candidacy.

LESSON 80

NETWORK WITH IMPACT

When you are networking, it is critical that you are proactively networking and you don't just obtain contact information from the person you are networking with, but truly establish a relationship with them. Don't be the person who goes to a networking event and just looks to collect the most business cards from others. You have to begin by being willing to help the other individual you are networking with openly with no expectation of reciprocation. Think of it as every relationship has an emotional bank account and you are creating this account with someone and contributing to it. Then, when you have a need, you will have many in your network who will be willing to help you in return. It is critical that you treat each interaction as an "interview." Remember to brand yourself and establish a good impression with the individual you are networking with. Keith Ferrazzi's *Never Eat Alone* or Dale Carnegie's *How To Win Friends And Influence People* offer very sound advice for how to properly interact when networking. Ensure you get the individual's business card so that you have their contact information. Following the event, make sure you follow up with the individual and extend an invitation for them to connect with you on LinkedIn, hopefully scheduling either a phone call or possibly meet over coffee, but work towards evolving the new contact into a relationship.

LESSON 81

SCRIPT YOUR STORYTELLING

Even if you are an accountant, engineer or a web designer, you need to specialize in storytelling when you are in the midst of a career transition. The individual who can tell their story in the most compelling and engaging manner will win the job. In June 2018, Karl Smart and Jerry DiMaria of Central Michigan University published a scholarly journal article titled, "Using Storytelling As A Job Search Strategy." In their abstract, they write, "This article demonstrates and reinforces the role that well-told stories play in the success of the job-search process. Building on narrative theory, impression management, and an increased use of behavioral-based questions in interviews, well-crafted stories about work and educational experiences demonstrate skills applicants possess and convey them to interviewers in memorable ways." Take quality time well before a cup-of-coffee conversation, formal interview or group networking meeting to script your story. While the core elements of your script - your education, experience and successes - will stay the same, there will be times where you will need to deliver them in seconds in the form of an elevator pitch and other times over the course of an all-day interview to various decision makers. Your success in scripting your story will come in the sequence in which you tell your story and how effectively you integrate anecdotes and past successes that are most relevant to your audience. "An important part of storytelling is being able to confidently share your story about why you left your last job," commented Keith Green, a seasoned public relations and marketing communications professional. "Get it down and practice it just like your elevator speech. If you were laid off, there was a restructuring or ownership change that led to your departure, share it and move on. You will find that people are almost always sympathetic and a surprising number of them were in your shoes and can relate. The truth is, people won't care about the details and will want to focus on helping you." Success will also come in your delivery of your story - confident, articulate and engaging. From this day forward on your journey to the next opportunity in your career, transform yourself into the world's greatest storyteller. After all, you know the subject matter, your background and experience, better than anyone.[36]

---

36. https://journals.sagepub.com/doi/abs/10.1177/2329490618769877?journalCode=bcqe

LESSON 82

DEVELOP YOUR UNIQUE PERSONAL VALUE PROPOSITION

In an article for Harvard Business Review, Bill Barnett clearly communicates the importance for job seekers in developing their value proposition. "Your personal value proposition (PVP) is at the heart of your career strategy. It's the foundation for everything in a job search and career progression — targeting potential employers, attracting the help of others, and explaining why you're the one to pick. It's why to hire you, not someone else." What is something so unique about you that very few people can ever claim? What is something you accomplished at school or work which is one-of-a-kind? What is your talent or skill or hobby that will set you apart from every other candidate applying for the same job? As you pursue the next opportunity in your career, you want to contemplate and consider your unique personal value proposition that is not only unique, but communicates that it will deliver value to your future employer. Brands go through this exercise regularly as they market and advertise in an attempt to win over customers from the competition. For Domino's, for many years, it was that they would deliver your pizza in less than 30 minutes guaranteed. More recently for Bud Light, their claim is that their beer does not include corn syrup. With those two examples in mind, begin to ideate and construct your unique value proposition. It is not only something that you will you be able to articulate in your elevator pitch or formal interview, but it could also find its way onto your resume if you can write it in a pithy way that really pops in a relevant and meaningful way.[37]

LESSON 83

PREPARE YOUR POSITIONING STATEMENT

What does your personal and professional brand stand for? How can you deliver value to an organization? What makes you different than every other candidate that is interviewing for the exact same job? Just as a brand will develop a positioning statement to effectively communicate how their service or product fills a consumer need that the competition does not, you need to do the same. Take a step back and pause as you are racing ahead to your next job interview. After carefully reviewing the roles, responsibilities and metrics for success, if the employer provides them, start to write and develop your brand positioning statement. Like a consumer brand, debate and determine how your experience, skills and service will effectively fill a need at this potential employer that no other candidate can fill the way you can. The candidate that can develop and deliver that type of compelling position in their interview will differentiate themselves from the other finalists and improve their probability of being selected to fill the position.

LESSON 84

BUILD OUT YOUR BRAND NARRATIVE

" The best marketers are storytellers. After all, how many customers truly make purchasing decisions based on statistics or a cost-benefit analysis? Emotional appeals are the truest way to connect with customers, and stories are the most powerful method for doing so. This is what makes your brand's narrative so important." Like brands who market to consumers, you will need to develop your brand narrative. Most individuals who are competing for job opportunities don't consider themselves brands, but they are, and they need to market themselves like consumer brands. The way to do that is by developing your brand narrative. It consists of your history and your experience. It should pay homage to your upbringing and your values. It should also be forward-looking as well and offer a glimpse into your vision for innovation and transformation. It can include your unique value proposition and perhaps even your elevator pitch. You should take quality time to outline it at first and then write it out. While you most likely will never need to submit it in written form, every element of your brand narrative will be used as you participate in the interview process. There are no rules in developing your personal brand narrative, but by investing quality time in contemplating it and writing it, you will automatically, without even knowing it, start to develop the storytelling that you will deliver in a compelling and engaging manner when you conduct formal and informal interviews. With each interview, you will refine and evolve your narrative and one day, it will deliver the next opportunity in your career to you.[38]

---

38. https://www.chiefmarketer.com/the-power-of-brand-narrative-5-ways-to-create-it/

LESSON 85

PERFECT YOUR ELEVATOR PITCH

For *Forbes*, Nancy Collamer succinctly explains why every individual in the midst of a career transition needs to perfect their elevator pitch well before they ever get on the elevator... or attend a cocktail party of some other function. "If you're looking for a job, one of the first tasks on your to-do list should be crafting an ideal 'elevator pitch.' It's the 30-second speech that summarizes who you are, what you do and why you'd be a perfect candidate. You should be able to reel off your elevator pitch at any time, from a job interview to a cocktail party conversation with someone who might be able to help you land a position." You are not always going to have the opportunity to explain and detail your life's work. In fact, there are many times where you will have less than a minute to impress someone enough into investing more time in you. This is where your elevator pitch comes in. Typically, at the conclusion of career support group meetings, everyone in attendance has 15-20 seconds to introduce themselves via their elevator pitch. The most compelling pitches are always the ones that are unique, different, engaging, clever and usually get a few laughs, while still delivering a clear and concise message as to what type of position the individual is pursuing. Think of your elevator pitch as speed dating. First, determine your ice breaker, a unique fun fact that will grab the attention of your audience. Then, follow it up with a substantive fact or past success and finally, bring it home with a concluding statement that articulates how you plan to deliver business building value in a specific role in a specific industry, category or even organization. Elevator pitches are not just for use in elevators. You may need it at every toss and turn of your career transition journey, so develop it and perfect it well before you ever have to use it.[39]

39. https://www.forbes.com/sites/nextavenue/2013/02/04/the-perfect-elevator-pitch-to-land-a-job/#1bb09ac51b1d

LESSON 86

BRANDING BEGINS WITH YOUR EMAIL ADDRESS

How can something as simple as your choice of email address impact your job search as well as have a significant impact on your network? An email address is important in today's digital marketplace. Your email address is literally the "key" that will provide access to contact and collaboration. There are two important aspects that you must consider when establishing your email address. The first is portability and the second is branding. For portability, we must avoid the pitfall of creating an email address that is specific to your carrier or internet supplier. An example of such would be johndoe@verizon.net. What happens if you move or decide to take advantage of a less costly carrier plan? Phone numbers are portable from carrier-to-carrier, but email addresses are not? The reason for this is if you ever change your carrier, you have now lost your digital identity and the ability for your network members to communicate with you. The second concern is branding and the image you are seeking to project. We suggest first name and last name @ email provider (example – Gmail, Yahoo, etc.). Over the years, we have received many emails that were either unprofessional and/or had started out well, but there must have been many John Doe's so they became johndoe9928@verizon.net. Imagine the chance of someone mistyping this email address and if they do, chances are they will just think you already found a job or are no longer interested instead of following-up with you further once they don't hear back. Also, we have seen candidates sink their candidacy because their email was not consistent with a professional image. We actually received a resume with beachboy69@hotmail.com and many other email addresses that just aren't professional in nature. Finally, many individuals today are concerned with ageism. Please do not use an email like johndoe@aol.com which would project that you haven't kept up with technology. So, in the end, suffice to say email addresses do matter, so take the time to create one that will be consistent with your branding and be an asset to you.

LESSON 87

MANAGE YOUR MEDIA PRESENCE

Effectively managing your media presence is a key factor of success for every job search. Most employers conduct a digital search of your owned media channels as part of their due diligence in the hiring process. When you start a job search, simply Google yourself. You want to learn if there is any information that comes back that can harm your candidacy. We have seen individuals who find out that someone else has their same name and unfortunately have done some bad things that would harm their candidacy if a potential employer confused the candidate for the individual who had committed the transgressions. If you find this, you can proactively alert a potential employer that this situation exists and ensure and possible share evidence that it is not you and hopefully prevent it from harming your candidacy. Today, many individuals are open and vocal about politics and other issues, but feel it is appropriate on a personal site such as Facebook. Our lives are now an open book, and many have strong opinions on politics, current events and even sports. So, do yourself a favor as there is such a small difference between the candidates that the hiring manager is considering for filling the opportunity and ensure there is nothing out there digitally to hurt your candidacy or give your opponents the edge in selection over you. We have seen candidates not selected because of personal information that they have posted on their social media channels and the potential employer felt that it wasn't consistent with their image or brand. The bottom line is to be very selective and think through what you post and check what may come back in a search of your name at the beginning of a job search so you have enough time to address, in some cases clean up, what a potential employer will see so it doesn't tank your candidacy inadvertently.

LESSON 88

GET VISUAL WITH YOUR RESUME

Infographic resumes are a new approach to communicating your capabilities

If you want to differentiate yourself and your candidacy, you should consider creating a visual resume. However, we would like to add a disclaimer - as visual resumes are new some may be impressed with the creative and innovative format, but some, may not. Therefore, please also share a version of your resume in a traditional format. This way you don't run the risk of your candidacy being stopped as you "didn't meet the requirements."

Some great sources to research if you want to explore designing and developing a visual resume are:

- Visualize.me
- Visual CV
- Visual Resume
- Hashtag CV
- Ineedresu.me
- Kick resume
- Zety
- ResumeUp

- Resume by Canva
- Resumonk

LESSON 89

INVEST QUALITY TIME ON YOUR RESUME SPECS

You need to invest some quality time into creating a well thought through and comprehensive master resume. This master resume will contain the very important PARs (see Lesson 66) which will be critical to not only your resume but branding and interviewing activities as well. Then, as each opportunity arises you want to develop a quality submission and retain the version of the resume that you submitted to the specific opportunity identified in your master tracking sheet. Again, it is about quality, not quantity. Anyone can submit into the black hole the techniques outlined here in this book. If followed appropriately, you will get quality results (interviews, follow-up interviews, job offers). And, as importantly, you will minimize the time you have to spend in transition dealing with the uncertainty. Do this correctly and get it done and behind you and land successfully in a job you will enjoy sooner rather than later.

LESSON 90

PROACTIVELY REQUEST REFERENCES

There are two types of references - the first is one you can do proactively and have on your LinkedIn Profile as a recommendation and the second is an individual you provide directly to a potential employer at their request that they can contact. You should proactively seek out and have several individuals provide recommendations on your LinkedIn profile. This will differentiate you from other LinkedIn profiles that don't have recommendations and if you work with those who are willing to provide you a recommendation you can work with them to address different aspects that will help proactively validate some of your competencies and capabilities. We have seen some instances where recruiters and potential employers simply accepted the recommendations instead of requesting and contacting references. Additionally, you need to collaborate with your references to effectively leverage your relationship:

- Gain their agreement to serve as a reference on your behalf

- Review any opportunity that you will supply them as a reference in advance recapping the opportunity, who it is with, and why you would make a great candidate

- Keep them informed through each stage of the process so they understand and can be prepared and anticipate the contact reaching out

- Remember to thank them for their support regardless of the outcome and offer to reciprocate on their behalf if ever needed

LESSON 91

READY YOUR RESEARCH

"Are you looking for a way to stand out in your next job interview? While an impressive resume and work experience are helpful, a key factor that many interviewees overlook is researching your employer. When you walk into an interview with an understanding and knowledge of what the company does and how you could fit a specific need, you become relevant. You stand out." This excerpt from a blog post could not state any better the critical importance research must play in your job prospecting strategy. Whether you conducted extensive research or not as part of your past role and responsibilities, it should be one of your primary focuses now. From conducting initial research about past classmates and colleagues to researching job openings and opportunities, research should consume a significant amount of your time during your transition second only to networking. In fact, once you have uncovered an opportunity and are invited to compete for it, that's when the real research just gets started. From the moment you secure a formal or even informational interview, you need to start to dial-up your depth of research. The moment you get an interview on the calendar, you need to research everything about that individual - where did they go to college, where did they work prior to their current role, what type of content do they post on social media, what types of activities do they participate in outside of work, have they been quoted or featured in the media? Even search for videos of them presenting or conducting media interviews to better understand their verbal communication style and the types of messages they prioritize and deliver. You then need to conduct the same kind of due diligence on the company they work for - who are their clients, who is their competition, what have they been in the news for lately, what are the most pressing concerns in their industry or category? Then, and only then, will you have conducted enough research to have prepared yourself to achieve success. However, don't fool yourself by thinking a couple of Google searches is conducting in-depth research. You can never conduct enough research.[40]

---

40. http://blog.post.edu/2018/07/have-an-interview-6-reasons-why-research-is-key/

LESSON 92

PRIORITIZE PREPARING FOR YOUR INTERVIEW

E ffective preparation for your interview will be critical to your success:

- Thoroughly review the job specifications and clearly communicate the value that you will deliver

- Work through your PARs specific to the needs of this position

- Research the organization thoroughly and develop some insightful questions for those who will be interviewing you

- Have a draft of your "Thank You" letter so you can fit in specifics from the interview to again strengthen your candidacy. If you are interviewed by more than one person, personalize each thank you letter to each individual

- Ensure you know exactly where you are traveling to for the interview, and when possible, do a dry run the weekend prior to the location

- Leave extra time to travel to the interview as there is only "on-time" or late, and you never want to be late. You have only one chance to make a strong first impression and being late is not going to help you do that

- Don't discuss anything regarding the interview with anyone (recruiter, family member, etc.) until you are off-premise of the employer and out of earshot of anyone that can be associated with the employer

- Pick up a book on body language so that you can read non-verbal cues from the interviewer as you are interacting with them

- Practice interviewing techniques and questions in advance of the interview, but during the interview carefully interact, listen intently and follow cues from the interviewer

- If you have been able to make a contact at the employer through your network, ask your contact about the attire appropriate for interviewing- formal suit or business casual

- Remember that everything you bring with you to the interview helps the interviewer form an opinion of you. If you are an older candidate and are saying you are tech savvy and pull out a flip phone, it's not going to go over well

LESSON 93

ASK HIGH-QUALITY QUESTIONS

In a column titled, "10 Ridiculously Smart Questions You Should Ask In A Job Interview," Rachel Weingarten writes, "You've been so busy preparing to answer questions, that you're forgetting to show the curiosity that lets interviewers see what you really want to know. After all, even if every single one of your responses are flawless and on point, by not asking a question or two of your interviewer, you run the risk of coming across as generic." However, you can't just ask any question or two. You need to ask smart, thought-provoking, high-quality questions.

- As your organization competes for new business and clients, how do you articulate why prospects should choose your firm over the others?

- With the marketplace evolving so rapidly, what specific areas will the company focus on over the next several years to continue to innovate and transform?

- What's the biggest opportunity for growth over the next few years?

- In your own words, how would you describe your company's culture?

- How will you measure success of the new hire in this role a year from now?

- What keeps you up at night with respect to your role, responsibilities and delivering business impact and value?

These types of high-quality questions are smart and strategic in nature. They are also the type of questions that transform a job interview into a collaborative conversation. Often, the candidate who is selected for the job is the one who those conducting the interviews had the most compelling "conversation" with, not the most compelling interview. A senior marketing communications executive remarked, "I'm convinced a candidate's questions, not answers, separate them from the pack. By asking insightful questions, the candidate is inviting the interviewer to engage in a more authentic conversation that reveals what it would be like to work with this candidate."[41]

41. https://www.theladders.com/career-advice/questions-job-interview

LESSON 94

PHONE INTERVIEWS: ARTICULATE YOUR ATTITUDE

Phone interviews are good and bad. They are good in that they just basically gave you a gift of making the interview an open book test and bad in that you need to be prepared and have an understanding of the nuances of a phone interview from an in-person interview so that you can take advantage of these differences and use them for your success. Many label the phone interview the "ironing board interview" and that's because what many do is set up their materials on an ironing board in front of a mirror. The ironing board is long and narrow and will allow you to lay out several reference materials in an order and way you can quickly lay your hands on them. By doing this in front of a mirror, the suggestion is that you smile the entire time as having the visual feedback helps you to remember and come across better. Also, standing while you do the interview has been proven to help you project your voice better and make a better impression. One point to remember as you cannot see the interviewer and they can't see you, it is critical that you employ great active listening skills and listen for tone in their responses and if you hear or need a question explained further remember to do so rather than potentially looking like you don't know the answer. The bottom line is that with a phone interview, the potential employer can not see you, your body language or how you are dressed. So, they are making their decision based on your articulation and confidence as well as the answers and content you deliver. Finally, always remember that technology plays a critical role in a phone interview. If you have a poor phone connection, it may eliminate you from the process because that poor cell phone connection will not allow you to articulate with confidence. Test out your connection in advance and proactively think through a backup alternative in case problems arise.

LESSON 95

SCRIPT YOUR SKYPE SESSION

Through this book, we stress the importance of conducting extensive research to prepare for every interview. However, a Skype session requires some additional considerations:

- Plan where you intend to physically take the Skype call and ensure that the background (the wall behind you) aligns with the image that you want to project and also ensure the lighting is appropriate

- Set-up a dry run with your laptop and ensure that it's positioned so the screen is looking directly at you not low or high

- During your dry run, conduct an actual dress rehearsal, putting on the clothing that you intend to wear during the interview so that you can see how it displays

- Make sure all pop-ups like instant messenger and mail notification are temporarily disabled on your device so that they don't interfere with your session

- Conduct a test interview with someone using the Skype service to ensure that you have tested and ironed out any technical issues or connection problems

- Even after you prepare and script your Skype session, you have to remember that the interviewer will be driving the interview so be prepared and ready to adapt as they conduct the interview

- If the meeting invite indicates that a product will be used like Webex, Zoom or something similar, make sure you check that the device you plan to use meets the required system requirements and download that application in advance and gain some familiarity with the product so you can navigate it seamlessly during the interview.

LESSON 96

BE THE GREATEST INTERVIEWEE

I f it's been a while since you interviewed for a position (interviewing candidates to consider hiring them doesn't count) or if you are new to interviewing, there are numerous things that will help you. Seek out resources to prepare you: engage a career coach, tap your university alumni office who supply interview training, or engage a job search or networking group that offers interview preparation advice and training – TAKE ADVANTAGE OF IT! Also, you can ask friends, family or contacts if they are hiring managers and most will be willing to run you through a mock interview and provide you feedback. You can also video the interview so you can then watch it and do your own self critique identifying strengths and weaknesses to work on. You must do your homework. Research the employer and have good questions prepared that you can ask. Review the job requisitions extensively and your T Letter so you understand the evidence you provided as to why you were a match so you can speak to the PARs that you shared. Make sure when you close your interview that you reinforce your interest in the position and ask what the next steps and timeline are for a final decision. This is critical for your follow-up. Immediately following the interview, compose a well-thought through personalized "Thank You" note to send to each interviewer. If a recruiter was involved, once you have left the interview and the potential employer's premises are in a place where you have privacy outside of the employer's offices or immediate surroundings, call the recruiter and debrief them on how the interview went.

LESSON 97

USE BODY LANGUAGE TO YOUR ADVANTAGE

Understanding body language is another critical skill needed during your job search and throughout life. It is critical that you purchase a book on this topic and truly understand the fundamentals of body language prior to your interview. As you are speaking with the interviewer, use good eye contact. Also, upon meeting the interviewer provide a strong and confident handshake upon meeting them. As you are answering questions, it is important that you carefully study the interviewer's body language and maintain eye contact. If they seem to be growing disinterested with your response, you may not be on point, or your answer may be too long. Remember to be concise. Think of yourself conducting a three-minute live television interview where you need to answer each question in concise sound bites. If the interviewer seems frustrated or distracted, you may want to be proactive and let them know that you can wait or step outside their office if they have something urgent that they need to attend to immediately. This may make a significant difference. If they are distracted, they may not even remember interviewing you. Bring copies of your resume and T Letter and offer to provide them as the interviewer may not have them and it shows you are prepared. Be concise in your responses. If the interviewer wants to delve further, they will ask. If not, your initial response delivered the answer to the question they asked.

PART 5

CONTINUE TO NETWORK, PREPARE AND GIVE BACK

LESSON 98

NEVER STOP NETWORKING

W e would be all be multi-millionaires one day if we trademarked a line for bumper stickers and t-shirts that read, "Help, I'm Networking and I Can't Stop!"

So many individuals who are out of work, learn the importance of networking while they are in a career transition and in the job search mode, but then fall back to their former ways and don't network once they start their new job. They often claim that they have too much on their plate and use it as an excuse. However, there has never before been such a rate and volume of change in business due to digital transformation as there is today. This is causing major disruptions in all industries. The way in which business is done is literally changing. With these disruptions, we are the ones who are usually bearing the brunt with employers going out of business, merging, consolidating and divesting. It is more important now than ever in our history that you dedicate time to growing and strengthening your network. Additionally, many families are facing higher costs due to increases in taxes, prices, education and insurance. Thus, individuals and families don't have the financial buffer they once had. Therefore, please follow these two best practices:

- After securing a new job, put your networking competency to work at your new employer with new colleagues, consultants and preferred vendors

- Outside of your new job, stay involved in attending professional associations, give back to the networking groups that helped you, attend expo events and grow contacts and nurture relationships

LESSON 99

UNSPECTACULAR PREPARATION WILL BE THE KEY TO YOUR SUCCESS

Now that you have secured your next career opportunity, the work is really just beginning. Just as you prepared extensively for every informal meeting and formal interview by conducting significant research, continue to take that approach in advance of your official start date and every day of your new assignment. Now, your research should focus on your company, the competition, the industry and the responsibilities of your new position and the position above you. Ask your new manager to share any information in advance as you would welcome the opportunity to begin reviewing it and preparing for your new opportunity

There are two great books to consider making the most of your new opportunity:

- *The First 90 Days: Proven Strategies for Getting Up to Speed Faster and Smarter, Updated and Expanded* by Michael D. Watkins

- *The New Leader's 100-Day Action Plan: How to Take Charge, Build or Merge Your Team* by George Bradt, Jayme A. Check and Jorge Pedraza

LESSON 100

MAKE THE MOST OF YOUR FIRST 100 DAYS ON THE JOB AND BEYOND

Wow! I hated networking and now that I landed my new job, I can't wait to just relax.

Buzz – wrong!

Now, more than ever, it's important to continue networking with those people in the new organization that you just joined. Network with all those you meet at your new firm. Connect with coworkers, those you meet from other organizations, stakeholders, managers, executives, consultants, and even vendors. Publish content that demonstrates your thought leadership but make sure it is consistent with your firm's goals, objectives and positions. Continue your networking activities outside of work that helped you land the position.

Set a career plan of where you want to be in five to 10 years with measurable goals you want to achieve. Commit to continuous learning. "It was critical not to just get the job, but immediately blow the doors off for my new employer so they know that they undoubtedly made the best decision," said PJ Brovak, a marketing communications professional. "As a result, I have already been positively asked to take on more responsibilities and have set myself up for success with the organization." Technology is disrupting every facet of business including how it is getting done. We all must become lifelong learners. Relying on a college degree and learnings that are years in the past will no longer be enough. Keep a close eye on innovation and determine how your position will be transformed by it. Automation will be the source of greatest change in the future and we will all experience it, so embrace it and learn how to exploit it for the benefit of your career.

LESSON 101

PAY FORWARD WHAT YOU LEARNED

"When you get where you're goin'

Don't forget turn back around

Help the next one in line

Always stay humble and kind"

-Tim McGraw

Remember the earlier statements on building that emotional bank account when you network. We tell everyone that we help that their network is the only rainy day insurance policy any of us have when, and if, we find ourselves in a job search. Therefore, continue to network each day. Help everyone you can when you come across those in need. Your help can be everything from as little as referring them to a networking group, to accepting their LinkedIn connection to endorsing skills to writing recommendations and serving as a reference to helping them with their resume to running them through a mock interview. "I will never say no to helping someone in need no matter how busy or occupied I might be," said PJ Brovak, a marketing communications veteran. "I am thankful for the hundreds, yes hundreds, of people who invested their time in me. And I always tell those individuals I help that you never know when I might need to call on them in the future for some reason." If we live our lives by consistently making daily deposits into the emotional bank account with those who we encounter and grow and nurture relationships with those contacts, we will each be rewarded with a stronger network that will be there for us when we need it most. Brovak added, "And when you hear of the success that someone has had and realize that you might have played even just a small part of it, there is not a more rewarding feeling."

FINAL THOUGHTS

If you are currently unemployed and experiencing you own unique career transition, we hope that you found value in the lessons, advice, recommendations and insights in this book and that you are able to apply them immediately to your journey to the next opportunity in your career.

At the beginning of this book, we highlighted that it was inspired by career support networking groups like The Breakfast Club NJ and the incredible individuals who attend the group meetings seeking collaboration and content to help them with their job search. If you have never attended a career support networking group in your area, conduct some research and locate one near you. By attending their next meeting, you will open the door to new opportunities and possibilities not to mention dozens of new members in your professional network. Most importantly, like us, you will leave those meetings inspired, energized and reinvigorated to charge forward in your job search with an even more informed and strategic mindset and approach.

Always remember that this book is just one small piece of a positive movement of family, friends, colleagues, classmates, and even strangers you have yet to meet who are all mobilizing to lend their assistance and support.

Best wishes for tremendous success in securing your next job and even greater success once you start that job!

ABOUT THE AUTHORS

MARK BEAL

Before co-authoring *Career In Transition: 101 Lessons To Achieve Job Search Success*, Mark Beal served as a brand marketer for nearly 30 years, developing and executing marketing and public relations campaigns for category leading companies and brands. During that time, he created campaigns around such major sports and entertainment platforms as the Olympic Games, Super Bowl, World Series, US Open Tennis and The Rolling Stones.

Mark experienced his own career transition when he was invited to be an adjunct professor in the School of Communication and Information at Rutgers University in 2013. Mark has since been appointed as the university's first full-time Professor of Public Practice in Public Relations.

It was Mark's students who inspired him to write his first book, *101 Lessons They Never Taught You In College*, which was published in 2017 and his second book, *101 Lessons They Never Taught You In High School About Going To College*, which was published in 2018. Both books are available for purchase on Amazon.

101 Lessons They Never Taught You In College led to Mark being invited by career support networking groups in New Jersey and Pennsylvania to speak to individuals who were experiencing a career transition. It was these individuals who inspired Mark to co-author this book with Frank Kovacs.

Mark collaborates daily with Gen Z students which led to him authoring *Decoding Gen Z: 101 Lessons Gen Z Will Teach Corporate America, Marketers & Media*, which has captured the attention of media, marketers and employers nationwide as the oldest Gen Zers join the workforce and the entire Gen Z cohort becomes the primary focus of corporations and brands.

Mark brings his 101 Lessons to life via his podcast series, 101 Lessons in Leadership. In each podcast episode, Mark interviews a leader and delves into the mentors who inspired them as well as the lessons in leadership and life that they share with their current followers. The podcast episodes can be listened to for free by simply going to www.101lessonspodcast.com.

ABOUT THE AUTHORS

FRANK KOVACS

Frank Kovacs has been a technology business executive for more than 30 years leading and directing large, complex, global operations and transformations for some of the largest Fortune 100 firms as well as NASA.

Frank has been recognized as recipient of the Gartner CIO Choice Award, Visionary Award from Business Finance Magazine & Internet World, and the Ovation Award at Comnet. Frank was named a visionary for his 12 years of work at AT&T Bell Labs and has a patent for Smart Card Technology.

Following the attacks of September 11, 2001, Frank wanted to help those who lost their jobs due to the tragedy and formed a group, The Breakfast Club NJ (TBCNJ). More than 18 years later, TBC-NJ has grown to more than 6,000 members and is the premier job search and career networking group in the New York/New Jersey region. As TBCNJ extensively leverages social media, many of the job posts and career transition advice routinely go viral and TBCNJ has helped more than 9,000 individuals secure jobs all with a "pay-it-forward" volunteer approach.

Frank is very proud to capture many of the learnings from 18 years of TBCNJ and share them through this book in hopes that even more people will be helped with their respective job search as we all work through the challenges of today's digital disruption and reskilling.

Frank is a lifelong resident of South River and East Brunswick, New Jersey where he lives with his wife, Laurie, daughter, Julianna, and their German Shepherd, Minnie.